New Edition

Viewfinder

Topics

South Africa

The Rainbow Nation at the Cape

compiled and edited
by
Claudia Drawe

Langenscheidt

Berlin · München · Wien · Zürich · New York

Viewfinder

Topics

Unterrichtsmaterialien für die Sekundarstufe II

South Africa

The Rainbow Nation at the Cape

Herausgeber:
Prof. em. Dr. Dr. h.c. Dr. h.c. Peter Freese

Autorin:
Dr. Claudia Drawe

Projekt-Team:
Dr. Martin Arndt, Münster
Prof. Dr. Mita Banerjee, Siegen
David Beal, M. A., Bochum
Cornelia Becker, Bremen
Dr. Peter Dines, Cert. Ed., Ludwigsburg
Prof. i. R. Dr. Hanspeter Dörfel, Ludwigsburg
Prof. Dr. Sabine Doff, Frankfurt / Main
Dr. Claudia Drawe, Essen
OStR Dieter Düwel, Castrop-Rauxel
Prof. em. Dr. Dr. h.c. Dr. h.c. Peter Freese, Paderborn
Dr. Carin Freywald †
Dr. Christine Gottstein-Strobl, Eichstätt
Jennifer von der Grün, B. A., Dortmund
OStR Ulrich Imig, Wildeshausen
OStR Reimer Jansen, Oyten-Sagehorn
Dr. Michael Mitchell, M. A., Reken und Warwick
Prof. Dr. Michael Porsche, Paderborn
StD i. E. Detlef Rediker, Lippstadt
StD Dr. Peter-J. Rekowski, Kirchhain
StD i.K. Peter Ringeisen, M. A., Amberg
Karl Sassenberg, Münster
StD Henning Scholz †
StD Dr. Annegret Schrick, Essen
OStR Ekkehard Sprenger, Kiel
StR Susanne Stadler, Wiesbaden
OStD Dr. Dietrich Theißen †
Donald Turner, M. A. †
Prof. Dr. Laurenz Volkmann, Jena
Philip Wade, M. A., Cert. Ed., Amberg

Verlagsredaktion: Dr. Beatrix Finke
Visuelles Konzept, Layout und Produktion: Barbara Slowik, Atelier S., München

www.langenscheidt.de/viewfinder

Umwelthinweis: Gedruckt auf chlorfrei gebleichtem Papier.

1. Auflage 2009

Printed in Germany
ISBN: 978-3-526-51068-0

09011

Contents

* Titles provided by the editor

South Africa

Today's South Africa consists of nine provinces: the Western Cape, the Eastern Cape, the Northern Cape, the Free State, Limpopo, Gauteng, Mpumalanga, North-West and KwaZulu-Natal.

Its landscape is as diverse as its population: from grassy hills to semi-desert, you will find a great variety of scenery, plants and animals.

In the Kruger National Park you can meet what is known as the "Big Five": elephants, lions, leopards, rhinoceroses and buffaloes.

South Africa's constitution is one of the most progressive in the world.

South Africa is a multicultural society with eleven official languages. Among them are English, Xhosa, Zulu, Sotho and Afrikaans. "Unity in Diversity" is an important slogan in the country. South Africa has about 47 million inhabitants with different religious beliefs and cultures.

Facts and Figures

Apartheid means "separateness". It was a political system in South Africa from 1948-1994. The word is a synonym for racial segregation. All parts of life, public and private, were affected by this policy. It meant that people of different "races" could not go to the same school or sit on the same bench.

The three biggest and best known cities are Johannesburg in Gauteng, Durban on the coast in KwaZulu-Natal and Cape Town in the Western Cape. The cities are growing immensely as people try to escape the poverty of rural areas and many Africans from other countries like Zimbabwe or the Sudan seek refuge in South Africa.

Terms to refer to parts of the population:

Whites: this term refers to Afrikaners and English speaking South Africans, but also includes other immigrants from Europe like the Portuguese or the Greek among others.
Blacks: is often used synonymously for all non-whites.
Afrikaners: Afrikaners are the descendants of the first Dutch, French and German settlers of the Cape. They were called "boers" in the past, but today this term is no longer used because it is derogatory.
English speaking South Africans: descendants of the British settlers at the Cape.
Coloured: people of a mixed heritage.
Indians/Asians: Indians were brought to South Africa in the 19th century either as indentured labourers who worked on the sugar cane farms or as so-called "passenger Indians" who paid their own ship passage and were merchants or other professionals. The biggest Indian community outside India lives in KwaZulu-Natal. Other Asians are of Chinese descent and were also brought to South Africa as indentured labourers for the gold mines in the 19th and 20th century.
African: this term is used to refer to the black population. Nevertheless this group is very heterogeneous and can be subdivided into different ethnicities. The biggest groups are the Zulu and the Xhosa. Other ethnicities that you will find in South Africa are the Bushmen (descendants of the Khoisan), Swazi, Ndebele, Tswana, Tsongo, Basotho, Bapedi and Venda among others. Each ethnicity has its own history and tradition although they also share certain concepts and values.

Through urbanisation and interaction all these parts of South African society are in a constant process of change and adaptation, so that specific traditions are most prevalent in rural areas.

Claudia Drawe

1 The Khoikhoi at the Cape

When the Dutch East India Company (Vereenigde Oost-Indische Compagnie or VOC) and with it the first Europeans arrived at the Cape of Good Hope in 1652, they did not find an "empty" land as they claimed later on, but encountered and traded with the Khoikhoi who lived there. Little is known about the Khoikhoi and the San and their traditions. During apartheid this part of history was left out or was not considered important, but historians are now concentrating their research on the time before the arrival of Europeans to gather knowledge about these early inhabitants of the Cape and their way of life.

A drawing of the Khoikhoi by Samuel Daniell

When Europeans started settling at the Cape, they met two groups of indigenous people, the Khoikhoi and the San. The Khoikhoi were pastorals, meaning that they owned cattle or sheep and herded groups of these animals across the land. The San lived off the land as hunter-gatherers feeding on the plants they could find and hunting antelopes and smaller mammals. The relationship between Khoikhoi and San shifted frequently from peaceful coexistence to brief spells of war.

The instability in Khoikhoi society was further intensified by the nearby presence of San. Some San groups frequently attacked the Khoikhoi, sowing terror by firing off poisoned arrows normally used to hunt great game, and stealing and frequently slaughtering Khoikhoi livestock.

Yet many so-called San also lived peaceably in or on the fringes of Khoikhoi societies, serving Khoikhoi as hunters, guides, or spies and soldiers in time of war. Khoikhoi hired some as herders and took some as wives. In many areas, notably the southwestern Cape, the boundary between Khoikhoi and San became increasingly unclear. Newly impoverished Khoikhoi were often called San, and San who had prospered were absorbed into Khoikhoi lineages and polities. (Hermann Giliomee / Bernard Mbenga: *New History of South Africa,* Cape Town: Tafelberg, 2007, p. 21.)

The term "San" was given to the hunter-gatherers by the Khoikhoi, while the Dutch settlers referred to them as "Bushmen". The Dutch called the Khoikhoi "Hottentots". Both terms are often used in historical documents. Nowadays the term "Khoisan" is also often used because both indigenous groups interacted and integrated with each other, so that a clear distinction became impossible.

The structure of Khoikhoi society is well illustrated by the following passage:

[T]he Khoikhoi were organised in approximately twelve chiefdoms that the Dutch called 'nations'. Some were ruled by male figures (called 'kings' or 'captains' by the Dutch), but others had no leaders above headmen of small clans.

Though Khoikhoi had no standing armies and no military leaders apart from their chiefs, they seem to have engaged in frequent wars. European observers were deeply impressed by their dexterity in battle and by their skilful use of weapons. Wars were often triggered by cattle theft, murders, and by the abduction of prominent women – provocations that led to vendettas that would smoulder and flare up over the generations. Khoikhoi fought pitched battles, using assegais, bows, stones and darts as offensive weapons; they massed their oxen together as defensive ramparts and drove them forward as flying wedges to gore and trample the enemy.

Such battles, though apparently not very bloody, often resulted in significant transfers of herds and flocks from the vanquished to the victors. In other cases – as, for example, when they faced Dutch soldiers armed with muskets – the Khoikhoi could resort to guerrilla tactics, characterised by swift and overwhelming attack [sic] on the enemy's herds. (Ibid., p. 20)

Animals were essential to Khoikhoi society, because they were a source of food (in this case of milk and meat), because they provided clothing, transport and were a symbol of wealth. This last point became very important because the livestock were more valuable for the Khoikhoi than the land itself since that was only used to feed the animals and thus seen as pasture. It did not belong to anyone specifically. For the Dutch the land itself was important and was fenced in and claimed as their own territory while the animals were solely seen as providing food. The issue of land ownership and the different perceptions of the importance of the land and livestock became crucial in the interaction between Khoikhoi and Europeans and led to wars in the 17th century. The VOC established the first settlement at the Cape and saw the Khoikhoi as providers of meat for the passing ships that sailed on to the Dutch colony of Batavia. At first the Khoikhoi agreed to barter their animals with the Dutch, but soon they either offered sheep or inferior beasts or asked for better prices. This annoyed the VOC, which reacted by organising expeditions into the interior, and led to them exploring more and more of the country. The mutual good relationship which had been established at the beginning deteriorated fast. The theft of cattle by both parties and the severe retribution meted out by the Europeans soured relationships between the VOC and the Khoikhoi, but the consequences for the Khoikhoi were more serious: loss of livestock and land. Being robbed of their way of life meant that they were forced to become labourers. In addition, their numbers were drastically reduced by a series of smallpox epidemics in the 18th century. Thus their position at the Cape was further weakened.

Bushmen paintings in the Cederberge, Western Cape

Info

VOC

VOC stands for "Vereenigde Oost-Indische Compagnie" and was a private commercial trading company. It was founded in 1602 and enjoyed a trading monopoly in the area east of the Cape of Good Hope which enabled it to become the largest company in the world in the 17th century. It was politically and economically very powerful, though it lost its power in the 18th century as a result of competition from English and French traders and because its personnel became corrupt. It was declared bankrupt in 1794.

Vocabulary

2 indigenous (adj.): indigenous animals, plants etc have always lived or grown naturally in the place where they are, as opposed to others that were brought there - **22 impoverished** (adj.): very poor - **24 lineage** (n.): /ˈlɪni-ɪdʒ/ *fml.* the way in which members of a family are descended from other members - **24 polity** (n.): *fml.* a particular form of political government organization, or a condition of society in which political organization exists - **55 vendetta** (n.): a quarrel which continues for a long time in which one group or person tries to harm another because they feel angry about something that happened in the past - **57 pitched battle** (n.): a battle between armies who have already chosen and prepared their positions - **59 rampart** (n.): here: a protective wall - **60 to gore** (v.): if an animal gores s.o., it wounds them with its horns or tusks - **63 vanquish** (v.): *literary* to defeat s.o. or s.th. completely - **81 pasture** (n.): land or a field that is covered with grass and is used for cattle, sheep etc. - **92 crucial** (adj.): something that is crucial is extremely important because everything else depends on it - **97 to barter** (v.): to exchange goods, works or services for other goods or services rather than money - **104 retribution** (n.): punishment for s.th. serious - **104 to mete out** (v.): if you mete out a punishment, you give it to s.o.

Explanations

Title: **Khoikhoi**: this term literary means "men of men". The Khoikhoi lived in the South Western Cape during the 15th century at the time when the Portuguese first rounded the Cape. The history of the Khoikhoi is largely unknown, but it is supposed that they first appeared some 2000 years ago in the area now occupied by Botswana and Namibia. They moved further south so that by AD 500 Khoikhoi groups were settled along the western, southern and eastern Cape coasts. - **Introduction**: **San**: The San are the earliest people to have lived in southern Africa. They were spread across the subcontinent and had an extensive knowledge of their environment. They lived in small bands. During the 18th and 19th century they were hunted down and nearly exterminated by white settlers. A small number of San survived in remote desert areas. - **57 assegai**: wooden spear - **96 Batavia**: This was the name that the Dutch gave to the Indonesian capital Jakarta. Batavia was founded on the ruins of the Javanese town by VOC governor general J.P. Coen in 1619.

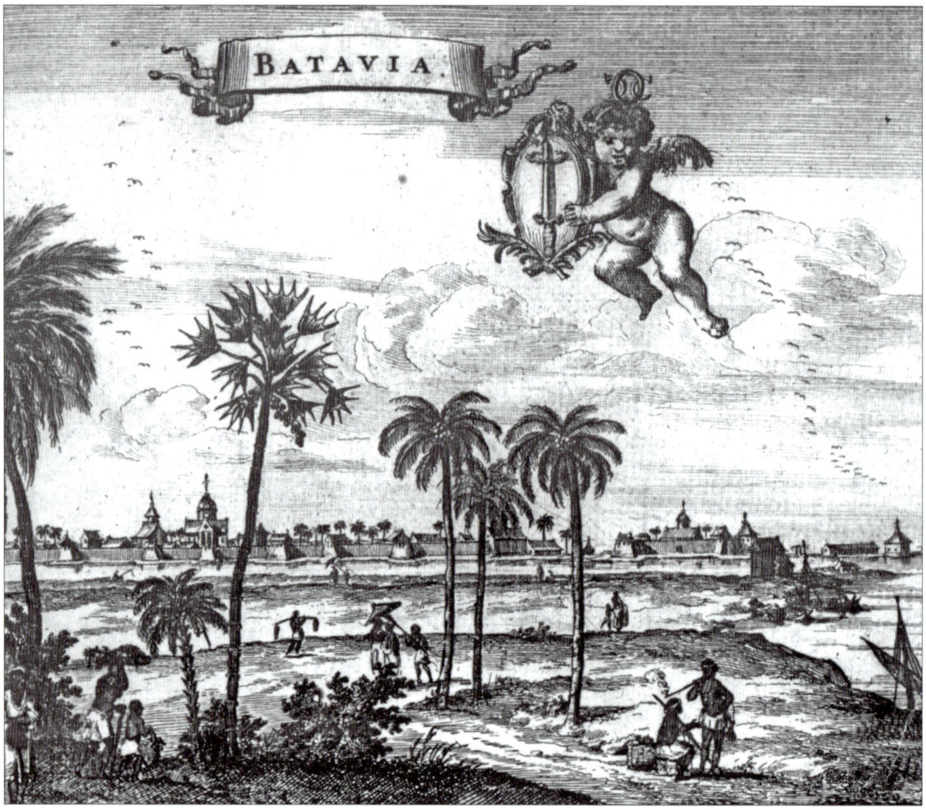

A historical view of Batavia

Awareness

1 Who were probably the first people to settle in the area where you live?

Comprehension

2 Which groups inhabited the area around the Cape before the 17th century?
3 What did the San and the Khoikhoi do for a living?

Analysis

4 What are the most significant traits of the relationship between the Khoikhoi and the San?
5 Why did the Europeans and the Khoikhoi clash?

Opinion

6 To what extent did Khoikhoi and Dutch society differ in the 17th century?
7 Why did the Khoikhoi lose their dominant position at the Cape? Give reasons.

Project

8 Find out more about the people who lived within the boundaries of today's South Africa before the Europeans arrived there. Who are they? How were their societies structured?

2

Claudia Drawe

The first settlement at the Cape

With the arrival of Jan van Riebeeck (see p. 10) in 1652 the situation at the Cape changed drastically. The Cape of Good Hope was no longer a refreshment station on the route to Batavia (see p. 8), but became a settlement that was dominated by the mercantile Vereenigde Oost-Indische Compagnie (VOC) and its interests (see p. 7). When the British occupied the Cape in 1795 and started to colonise it, the Cape underwent another major administrative change.

The first Europeans to round the Cape were the Portuguese in 1488, but they showed little interest in settling or trading at what they called "the Cape of Storms". Many ships used the Cape and Robben Island, the small island just off the shore of Cape Town, to refill their supply of fresh water and meat on their route to the East. Jan van Riebeeck arrived at the Cape on 6 April 1652 with three ships to establish a refreshment station where sailors could replenish their food and stock fresh water. This became essential because of the high mortality rate on the ships and diseases like scurvy that weakened the sailors. Jan van Riebeeck planted a vegetable garden and built a hospital to cater for the needs of passing ships. From these first beginnings the first settlement at the Cape developed.

At that time the Cape society consisted of the Khoisan, the VOC employees and slaves who were brought to the Cape from 1658 onwards. A few former VOC employees called "free burghers" were granted the right to own farms: The VOC set up strict rules for the Cape settlement and its inhabitants. It granted freedoms like owning a farm, but kept a strict regulation on where and for what price the free burghers could sell their goods and produce. This led to much discontent among them.

The settlement was highly dependent on the VOC and its policy. In 1689 about 180 Huguenots fleeing from the religious persecution in their own country were allowed to settle at the Cape. They founded and developed the wine industry of the country. This was an exception because the VOC was rather reluctant to allow new settlers into Cape society or encourage immigration to the Cape. This was a reason why the settlement did not grow rapidly, so that by the end of the 18th century only 15,000 free burghers lived in the colony.

In 1795 the British occupation of the Cape started. Its interest in the settlement was caused by their fear of growing French power in Europe. They did not want their enemy to capture the Cape first. In addition, the VOC had lost its power and was thus easily taken over by the British. Another reason was their awakening desire for colonies by other European countries.

Though the British guaranteed Dutch language rights and religious freedom, they also changed the administrative system at the Cape to their own liking.

The attitude of the commissioners towards the social structure of the colony was similarly shaped by their commitment to a free and efficient economy. The poor administrative record of the old system led the commissioners to believe that local bias and racial prejudice disqualified Cape Afrikaners from holding official positions. Conversely, they believed that the servile condition of the Khoikhoi and the free blacks inhibited productivity. The efficiency of Khoikhoi artisans when fairly remunerated and the success of a Khoikhoi farmer at Clanwilliam encouraged the commissioners to believe that, once granted personal liberty and security of property, the Khoikhoi and other people of colour would become "industrious farmers and respectable members of the community". This economic imperative was equally responsible – with missionary pressure and liberal humanitarianism – for bringing about the famous Ordinance 50 of 1828, one of the foundation stones of what came to be called "Cape liberalism". Ordinance 50 repealed existing oppressive laws, outlawed dubious varieties of labour contracts, and specifically reaffirmed the right of Khoikhoi and free people of colour to buy and own land and property on the same basis as white people.

Most important of all was the second clause. It stated that "no [Khoikhoi] or other free person of colour, lawfully residing in this Colony, shall be subject to any compulsory service to which other of His Majesty's subjects therein are not liable, nor to any hindrance, molestation, fine, imprisonment, or punishment of any kind whatsoever ... unless after trial in due course of law".

The Huguenot Museum in Franschhoek, Western Cape

The intention of Ordinance 50 may well have been to free up labour on Afrikaner farms for the use of British settlers in the Eastern Cape, but it did at least free the Khoikhoi from the threat of legally endorsed coerced labour under the pretence of antivagrancy laws. What Ordinance 50 did not do was to alleviate the economic plight of the coloured person. It distributed labour more fairly between English and Afrikaans [sic] and it protected the rights of the labourer to a certain extent, but the population nevertheless remained "free men who depend on employment for food" rather than independent producers. (Hermann Giliomee / Bernard Mbenga: *New History of South Africa,* Cape Town: Tafelberg, 2007, p. 89)

Jan van Riebeeck

Info

Jan van Riebeeck was born in 1619. He was a ship's surgeon, merchant and official of the VOC. He established a refreshment station at the Cape in 1652 and served as the first Commander of the Cape from 1652 to 1662. He died in 1677. Traces of the first settlement at the Cape can be found in Cape Town: the Castle and the Company's garden are examples for it. During apartheid and in history books he was often referred to as the "founding father of the country", implying that the history of South Africa starts with his arrival at the Cape. This approach is highly questionable. Today's history books include information about the first inhabitants of the Cape.

Vocabulary

9 replenish (v.): *fml.* to fill s.th. again or put new supplies into s.th. - **11 scurvy** (n.): a disease caused by not eating foods such as fruit and vegetables that contain vitamin C – **62 remunerate** (v.): *fml.* to pay s.o. for s.th. they have done for you - **70 ordinance** (n.): an order given by a ruler or governing organization - **85 hindrance** (n.): *fml.* the act of making it difficult for s.o. to do s.th. - **86 to molest** (v.): *old-fashioned* to attack and physically harm s.o. - **95 vagrancy** (n.): the criminal offence of living on the street and begging from people - **96 to alleviate** (v.): to make s.th. less painful or difficult

Explanations

19 free burghers: former officials of the VOC who were given land to farm. The term was also used for all white people at the Cape. The relationship between free burghers and the VOC was sometimes tense due to the economic restrictions by the VOC. - **26 Huguenots**: French protestant refugees who left their country because their religion was declared illegal and settled at the Cape between 1688 and 1700. - **53 commissioners**: the British government appointed officials to investigate conditions at the Cape. The commissioners at the time mentioned were J.T. Bigge and W. Colebrooke. - **58 Afrikaner**: see p. 5 - **63 Clanwilliam**: town in the northern part of the Western Cape - **98 Afrikaans**: Afrikaans is a language that evolved from Dutch spoken in the 17th century and its creolisation by languages spoken by slaves, Khoikhoi, Portuguese and coloureds. It developed into a separate language in the 19th century.

Awareness

1 What do you know about the trade routes of the Europeans to India/Asia? Draw a map of these routes.

Comprehension

2 Why did the Europeans trade with Asian countries?
3 Which goods were exchanged?
4 Who settled at the Cape?
5 Describe Cape society and its structure in the 17th and 18th century.
6 What were the functions and the effects of Ordinance 50?

Analysis

7 What was the Cape's function in the first place?
8 What did the British change?

Opinion

9 How did the settlers react to these changes? Explain why the settlers reacted as they did.

Project

10 Find out more about slavery at the Cape.
Where did the slaves come from?
What were they needed for?
How did slavery shape society at the Cape?

3

Hermann Giliomee / Bernard Mbenga

Moving northwards – The Great Trek*

The growing tension between the British colonists and the Afrikaner farmers (see pp. 9f.) led to what is known as the Great Trek. Groups of Afrikaners got together and decided to move northwards and away from the Cape Colony. The reasons for this movement were manifold as the text will show. – Hermann Giliomee / Bernard Mbenga: *New History of South Africa* (Cape Town: Tafelberg, 2007), pp. 108-111.

The Voortrekkers used ox wagons on their journeys

Two streams of Afrikaner migrants left the Colony in the second quarter of the nineteenth century. The first was an emigration of people called trekboers, who moved across the border as individual families in search of better pasture; the others moved in trek parties and emphasised political issues. They would later be called Voortrekkers.

Their trek was a bold and dramatic response to a political crisis that had engulfed the eastern and northeastern districts of the Cape Colony from the mid-1820s to the end of the 1830s. It was a fairly orderly mass rebellion against a breakdown of security that the participants considered intolerable. Many also moved because all the land in the frontier districts had been taken. Thus the trek was also a solution to a material problem. [...]

Lack of land

A shortage of land had long been acute on the frontier, and the situation had steadily worsened between 1812 and the mid-1830s. During the eighteenth century the farmers, or their sons or sons-in-law, moved on to new land after pastures had been exhausted. But that depended on 'free' land – that is, land that could be taken without any cost and converted into a loan farm.

Early in the nineteenth century this way of life came to an end. In 1813 the British abolished the familiar loan farm system, and introduced a system of perpetual quitrent tenure. There was a long delay in the issue of title deeds, farms were wrongly surveyed and in some cases corrupt surveyors pocketed the money.

From the early 1830s the government returned land applications with a note that it could no longer issue land. The market price of established farms rose sharply. People left the colony because they wished to obtain new land to practise subsistence farming along traditional lines.

There seemed to be abundant free land beyond the colonial borders. By the mid-1820s migrant farmers, called trekboers in the north and northeast, were already expanding beyond the border, and severe droughts spurred them on. Initially they made humble requests to cross the border only as a temporary relief measure. But, by the end of the 1820s, these trekboers were no longer asking permission, and simply informing the authorities in Graaff-Reinet that they were crossing the boundary. Many trekboers sold their farms and moved to the other side of the border.

Lack of labour

Labour had long been a critical issue. The farms were large and homesteads were six or seven kilometres apart, with no fences to keep cattle in. Particularly after Ordinance 50 there was a severe shortage of cattle herders. Farmers did not pay their servants well. Dr Philip believed that the farmers would attract labour if they offered good cash wages, but Afrikaner colonists were much slower than their British counterparts to switch to commercial farming and cash wages. These farmers with sufficient land hoped to retain labourers by displaying a benign paternalism, particularly by allowing servants to keep some stock. However, the growing pressure on the land meant that few farmers could provide the Khoikhoi with enough land for their own stock.

Ordinance 50 of 1828 freed the Khoikhoi from all curbs on their movement, and they began moving away in large numbers from the farms. [...] The loss of patriarchal authority over slaves or servants was an important reason why many trekkers left. Ordinance 50 proscribed the punishment of Khoisan labourers by masters. On 1 December 1834 the right to punish slaves, now called apprentices, was also abolished. Labourers, particularly slave apprentices after 1834, felt free to take their masters or mistresses to court. Several Voortrekker leaders had brushes with the law about punishing their slaves or servants. [...]

Lack of security

Another central reason for the trek was the grave insecurity on the frontier. In Tarka and other parts of the northeastern border, Bushmen bands had been stealing cattle. [...] Wandering parties moved across the frontier, stealing or begging for food.

Government agents could issue passes for short periods; those who wished to stay longer to work had to negotiate a contract. In reality the government was unable to control the influx. Most frontier burghers did not know how to cope with vagrancy and constant cattle theft; many had experienced heavy losses of flocks and herds, and some were afraid for their lives. [...]

Political marginalisation

Lack of land, labour and security were serious sources of discontent. Yet by themselves they are not enough to explain why not only landless people left the colony but also fairly wealthy farmers, who sold their farms cheaply. To understand this, their grievances about a lack of representation must be taken into account.

This was keenly felt because labouring classes were now on an equal footing with them. These feelings were rooted in the status distinctions of the VOC that were not formally racial. There was no developed theory of racism among the frontier farmers, or among Afrikaners in general, during the nineteenth century. [...]

A lack of representative bodies where they could voice their complaints was one of the important reasons why so many believed it was impossible to remain in the colony.

The Voortrekker Monument (1940), Pretoria

Info

Voortrekker leaders

The term "Great Trek" refers to different trek parties. The treks set out from different places at different times with more than 100 participants. The treks were led by brave trek leaders. One example for such a leader was Louis Tregardt (1783-1838). He trekked to Delagoa Bay (now Maputo in Mozambique) in 1836, where he died of malaria. Other well-known leaders were Hendrik Potgieter (1794-1852), Piet Uys (1797-1838) and Piet Retief (1780-1838). Hendrik Potgieter left the Cape Colony in 1834 and trekked northwards. He founded several towns, e.g. Potchefstroom. Piet Retief made his way over the Drakensberg range hoping to find fertile land. The Zulu under Dingaan were suspicious of his intention and believed that he wanted to attack them. They invited Retief and his men into their village *(kraal)* and killed them. Piet Uys left his home Uitenhage in 1837 and traveled to Natal and to the area that is now called Free State. He was killed in a battle with the Zulu.

The Great Trek became a myth of Afrikaner nationalism in the 20th century. The Trek was portrayed as a heroic deed of hard working and enduring people who had to fight British and African adversaries in order to gain their independence. They were understood as chosen people who had suffered the hardships of the Trek with the help of God.

Vocabulary

35 tenure (n.): the legal right to live in a house or use a piece of land for a period of time - **42 subsistence** (n.): a small amount of money or food that is just enough to survive - **48 to spur on** (v.): to encourage s.o. to try harder in order to succeed - **56 critical** (adj.): very important because what happens in the future depends on it - **66 benign** (adj.): kind and gentle - **66 paternalism** (n.): a system of controlling people or organizations, in which people are protected and their needs are satisfied, but they do not have any freedom or responsibility - **76 to proscribe** (v.): *fml.* to try to stop the existence of s.th. such as a political organization - **81 brush** (n.): here: a time when you only just avoid an unpleasant situation or argument - **100 vagrancy** (n.): the criminal offence of living on the street and begging from people

Explanations

33 loan farm system: it was introduced by the VOC in 1714. The farmers were given land for an annual fee of 24 rix-dollars. The range of the area controlled by the individual farmer was defined by a radius of a half-hour walk in every direction. - **35 quitrent**: a tax imposed by the government on freehold or leased land - **52 Graaff-Reinet**: town in the Eastern Cape - **59 Ordinance 50**: see pp. 9f. - **60 Dr John Philip** (1775-1851): Scottish missionary. He arrived at the Cape in 1819 and worked as a superintendent of the London Missionary Society. He was critical of the treatment of the Khoikhoi and a member of the anti-slavery society. - **69 Khoikhoi**: see p. 8 - **89 Bushmen**: see p. 6 - **115 VOC**: see p. 7

Awareness

1 Have you come across an event like the Great Trek in world history? Which one is it? Why did people move?

Comprehension

2 What are the differences between trekboers and Voortrekkers?

Analysis

3 Why did some farmers leave the Cape Colony?

4 To what extent was the British colonial system responsible for the Great Trek?

Opinion

5 Can you imagine why the Great Trek became a key event in historiography during apartheid? Give reasons for your opinion.

Project

6 Roughly at the same time as the Great Trek, other areas of South Africa were affected by the Mfecane, also called Difaqane (Sotho). Find out what the Mfecane is and what decisive impact it had on Africans.

Claudia Drawe

4 The battle for control – the South African War

During the 19th century the tension between the British and the Afrikaners grew with the expansion of the British Empire and the annexation of Natal in 1843, among others. A military conflict between the two groups became inevitable. With the discovery of diamonds in the 1860s and gold in the Witwatersrand reef, Transvaal, in 1886, the struggle for power and control over these resources escalated and led to the South African War, which is also known as the Anglo-Boer War.

The Boer republics, the Orange Free State and the Transvaal, declared war on Great Britain in October 1899 because they wanted to preserve their independence. They also hoped that they could influence the outcome of the war positively if they acted quickly and thus caught the British unawares whose troops in South Africa were weak in comparison and needed reinforcing for a full blown war. Another reason for the Boer republics to declare war was their hope that the fighting would spread into the other British colonies, namely the Cape and the Natal Colony, and thus cause havoc and confusion for the British Empire.

The British, on the other hand, thought that they could easily and swiftly win this war against "a mob or rough tribe of Boer riflemen" (Hermann Giliomee/ Bernard Mbenga: *New History of South Africa,* Cape Town: Tafelberg, 2007, p. 211). They underestimated their enemy greatly so that by the end of 1899 the so-called

Lord Frederick Roberts

Lord Horatio H. Kitchener

Boer commandos or troops could invade deep the British territory and lay siege to strategically important towns like Mafeking (in the north near the border of what is now Botswana) and Ladysmith in what is now KwaZulu-Natal.

The British reacted by sending in massive reinforcements. They also sent a new chief commander, Lord Roberts, and his chief of staff, Lord Kitchener, to South Africa who gave the war a new turn by implementing what was to become known as "scorched earth" tactics. This meant that the British forces acted against civilians by burning farms and crops and slaughtering livestock thus diminishing the food resources of their enemies. They hoped to weaken the supply and the morale of the Boer commandos by stripping them of the help and support from their families. Another measure used to crush Boer resistance was the establishing of concentration camps where mostly old people, women and children were kept in appalling living conditions. Many people died of malnutrition or diseases in the camps. Thus scorched earth tactics together with the implementation of concentration camps led to a serious rift between the two white groups in South Africa.

The Boer republics resorted to effective guerrilla warfare, so that the war dragged on for another two years. In 1902 both sides were exhausted by the war effort and decided to negotiate the end of the war. This led to the Treaty of Vereeniging and resulted in the loss of independence of the Boer republics in exchange for British help in reconstructing them. Though the rift between Boer and British increased because of the South African War, the Union of South Africa in 1910 unified the white population in practice and thus established its dominance over the black majority living in the country.

The South African War was one of the most costly for the British Empire. Beside the financial cost of 217 million pounds, 22,000 British and 7000 Boer soldiers lost their lives while 20,000 Boer civilians and about 20,000 Africans died during the war.

Vocabulary

5 to catch s.b. unawares: to happen or do s.th. in a way that s.o. was not expecting and so was not prepared for - **11 havoc** (n.): a situation in which there is a lot of confusion or damage - **24f. reinforcements** (n. pl.): more soldiers who are sent to an army to make it stronger - **27f. to implement** (v.): to take action or make changes that you have officially decided should happen - **49 rift** (n.): a situation in which two people or groups have begun to dislike or distrust each other, usually caused by a serious disagreement

Explanations

10 Cape and Natal Colony: In the 1890s the Cape Colony, Natal and Zululand were British territories, while Transvaal and the Orange Free State belonged to the Afrikaners (see p. 5). The territory of the Cape Colony matches today's Western, Eastern and Northern Cape taken together. Natal and Zululand are today's KwaZulu-Natal. Transvaal is now the provinces Limpopo, Mpumalanga and Gauteng. The Orange Free State is now called Free State. - **19 commandos**: This term was first used in the 17th century when free burghers (see p. 10) organised their own military units that were independent of the VOC's (see p. 7) control. The Voortrekkers (see p. 11) used the commando system against their African (see p. 5) enemies. Commando service was compulsory in the two Boer republics during the South African War. - **26 Lord Frederick Roberts** (1832-1914): Commander-in-Chief of the British forces in the South African

War until 1900. He then became Commander-in-Chief of the British Army from 1901-1904. - **26 Lord Horatio Herbert Kitchener** (1850-1916): Commander-in-Chief of the British forces from 1900 to the end of the South African War

Treaty of Vereeniging

The outcome of the negotiations between the British Empire and the two Boer Republics was the Treaty of Vereeniging. The following important agreements were included:

"The BURGHER Forces in the Field will forthwith lay down their Arms [...] and desist from any further resistance to the Authority of HIS MAJESTY KING EDWARD VII whom they recognise as their lawful SOVEREIGN. The manner and details of this Surrender will be arranged between Lord Kitchener and Commandant General Botha, Assistant Commandant General De la Rey, and Chief Commandant de Wet."

"The DUTCH language will be taught in Public Schools in the TRANSVAAL and the ORANGE RIVER COLONY where the Parents of the Children desire it, and will be allowed in COURTS of LAW when necessary for the better and more effectual Administration of Justice."

"The question of granting the Franchise to Natives will not be decided until after the introduction of Self-Government."

"As soon as conditions permit, a Commission [...] will be appointed in each District of the TRANSVAAL and ORANGE RIVER COLONY, under the Presidency of a Magistrate or Official, for the purpose of assisting the restoration of the people to their homes and supplying those who, owing to war losses, are unable to provide for themselves, with food, shelter, and the necessary amount of seed, stock, implements etc, indispensable to the resumption of their normal occupations."

"In addition to the above named free grant of three million pounds, His Majesty's Government will be prepared to make advances as loans for the same purposes, free of interest for two years, and afterwards repayable over a period of years with 3 per cent interest."

Explanations

Louis Botha (1862-1919): first prime minister of the Union of South Africa. Botha was an Afrikaner general in the South African War and negotiated the Treaty of Vereeniging. He favoured unity between Afrikaners and the British. - **Jacobus Hercules De la Rey** (1847-1914): Boer general and politician. He was against South Africa's participation in World War I and planned a rebellion to restore the independence of the two Boer republics. He was shot by a police patrol and thus became a hero for Afrikaner nationalists. - **Christiaan Rudolf de Wet** (1854-1922): Boer general and rebel. Like de la Rey he opposed South Africa's involvement in World War I. He was tried and imprisoned for his participation in the rebellion in 1914. In later years he distanced himself from politics.

Awareness

1 What is guerilla warfare?

Comprehension

2 Which strategies were used by the Afrikaners? Did they work? Give reasons for your opinion.
3 What is meant by "a mob of Boer riflemen" (ll. 14f.)?

Analysis

4 Explain scorched earth tactics. What results did they achieve?

Opinion

5 Do you think that the South African War finally united the two white groups? Give reasons for your opinion.

Project

6 Analyse the Treaty of Vereeniging (http://www.sahistory.org.za/pages/governence-projects/anglo-boer-wars/vereeninging.htm). Which rights did the Afrikaners maintain? Which advantages were given to the British?

5

Nelson Mandela

Long Walk to Freedom

The National Party came into power in 1948 and started to implement its ideology of apartheid. A series of laws was enacted to separate all South Africans into prescribed categories and to regulate contact between the racial groups. In fact, through this policy the party supported the white minority rule of the country, excluded the majority of the population from the political process and degraded them to cheap labourers. In the 1950s there still seemed to be a chance to stop this development towards a racially segregated and highly divided society. Many resistance movements tried to reverse and oppose the process through passive resistance. The Defiance Campaign in 1952 is an example. – Nelson Mandela, *Long Walk to Freedom* (London: Abacus, 1995), pp. 146f., 151-153, 159.

Protesters during the Defiance Campaign

We [leaders of the ANC] also discussed whether the campaign should follow the Gandhian principles of non-violence or what the Mahatma called satyagraha, a non-violence that seeks to conquer through conversion. Some argued for non-violence on purely ethical grounds, saying it was morally superior to any other method. This idea was strongly affirmed by Manilal Gandhi, the Mahatma's son and the editor of the newspaper *Indian Opinion,* who was a prominent member of the SAIC. With his gentle demeanour, Gandhi seemed the very personification of non-violence, and he insisted that the campaign be run along identical lines to that of his father's in India.

Others said that we should approach this issue not from the point of view of principles but of tactics, and that we should employ the method demanded by the conditions. If a particular method or tactic enabled us to defeat the enemy, then it should be used. In this case, the state was far more powerful than we, and any attempts at violence by us would be devastatingly crushed. This made non-violence a practical necessity rather than an option. This was my view, and I saw non-violence on the Gandhian model not as an inviolable principle but as a tactic to be used as the situation demanded. The principle was not so important that the strategy should be used even when it was self-defeating, as Gandhi himself believed. I called for non-violent protest for as long as it was effective. [...]

On that first day of the Defiance Campaign more than 250 volunteers around the country violated various unjust laws and were imprisoned. It was an auspicious beginning. Our troops were orderly, disciplined, and confident.

Over the next five months, 8,500 people took part in the campaign. Doctors, factory workers, lawyers, teachers, students, ministers, defied and went to jail. They sang, "Hey, Malan! Open the jail doors. We want to enter." The campaign spread throughout the Witwatersrand, to Durban and to Port Elizabeth, East London and Cape Town, and smaller towns in the eastern and western Cape. Resistance was beginning to percolate even in the rural areas. For the most part, the offences were minor, and the penalties ranged from no more than a few nights in jail to a few weeks, with the option of a fine which rarely exceeded £10. The campaign received an enormous amount of publicity and the membership of the ANC shot up from some 20,000 to 100,000, with the most spectacular increase occurring in the eastern Cape, which contributed half of all new members. [...]

The government saw the campaign as a threat to its security and its policy of apartheid. They regarded civil disobedience not as a form of protest but as a crime, and were perturbed by the growing partnership between Africans and Indians. Apartheid was designed to divide racial groups, and we showed that different groups could work together. The prospect of a united front between Africans and Indians, between moderates and radicals, greatly worried them. The Nationalists insisted that the campaign was instigated and led by communist agitators. The minister of justice announced that he would soon pass legislation to deal with our defiance, a threat he implemented during the 1953 parliamentary session with the passage of the Public Safety Act, which empowered the government to declare martial law and to detain people without trial, and the Criminal Laws Amendment Act, which authorized corporal punishment for defiers. [...]

We made many mistakes, but the Defiance Campaign marked a new chapter in the struggle. The six laws we singled out were not overturned; but we never had any illusion that they would be. We selected them as the most immediate burden pressing on the lives of the people, and the best way to engage the greatest number of people in the struggle.

Prior to the campaign, the ANC was more talk than action. We had no paid organizers, no staff and a membership that did little more than pay lip-service to our cause. As a result of the campaign, our membership swelled to 100,000. The ANC emerged as a truly mass-based organization with an impressive corps of experienced activists who had braved the police, the courts and the jails. The stigma usually associated with imprisonment had been removed. This was a significant achievement, for fear of prison is a tremendous hindrance to a liberation struggle. From the Defiance Campaign onward, going to prison became a badge of honour among Africans.

We were extremely proud of the fact that during the six months of the campaign, there was not a single act of violence on our side. The discipline of our resisters was exemplary.

Manilal Gandhi and his daughter (1946)

Info

The ANC

ANC stands for African National Congress and was founded in 1912 to oppose the growing tide of segregation. The organisation was called South African Native National Congress (SANNC) prior to 1923. At first its tactics took the moderate form of petitioning. A new generation influenced by African nationalism called for more active opposition to the state in the 1940s. As a result the ANC used passive resistance. It was banned in 1960, which led to a change of tactics to an armed struggle and an organisation in exile. Internationally it became a symbol of opposition to apartheid. It was legalised in 1990 and is still the leading party in South Africa.

Vocabulary

10 demeanour (n.): the way s.o. behaves or looks that gives you a general idea of their character - **23 inviolable** (adj.): *fml.* an inviolable right, law, principle etc is extremely important and should be got not rid of - **31 auspicious** (adj.): *fml.* likely to be successful - **36 to defy** (v.): to refuse to obey a law or rule, or refuse to do what s.o. in authority tells you to do - **41 to percolate** (v.): if information percolates among people, it is passed gradually from one person to another - **53 perturbed** (adj.): worried or annoyed because of s.th. that has happened - **64 martial law** (n.): a situation in which the army controls an area instead of the police, esp. because of fighting against the government - **92 hindrance** (n.): *fml.* the act of making it difficult for s.o. to do s.th.

Explanations

1 ANC: see p. 17 - **7 Manilal Gandhi**: was born in India in 1892 and was the second son of Mahatma Gandhi. He lived in South Africa with his family and joined his father's satyagraha struggle in 1910. He stayed in South Africa while his father returned to India. In the 1950s he joined the passive resistance struggle and the Defiance Campaign. He died in 1956. - **9 SAIC**: the abbreviation stands for South African Indian Congress. It was an organisation that was formed in 1920 to represent the interests of Indians in South Africa. It organised mass resistance campaigns. - **37 Daniel F. Malan**: was born in 1874. He was Prime Minister from 1948-1954 and put his National Party's policy of apartheid into practice. Malan died in 1959. - **57 African, Indian**: see p. 5

Awareness

1 Do you know of any other examples of passive resistance in modern history?

Comprehension

2 What kind of methods for passive resistance do you know?
3 What was the Defiance Campaign? Was it a success?
4 Why did going to prison become a badge of honour (l. 94 ff.)?

Analysis

5 Which ideologies influenced the Defiance Campaign?
6 Non-violent resistance is discussed at the beginning of the text. Which two approaches can you find? To what extent do they differ from each other?
7 What measures were taken by the apartheid government to react to oppositional movements?
8 What is Mandela's attitude towards passive resistance?

Opinion

9 How effective can passive resistance be? Give reasons for your opinion.
10 The main influence on the defiance campaign was Mahatma Gandhi's philosophy of passive resistance. To what extent can these campaigns be called passive resistance?

Project

11 Find out more about Mahatma Gandhi's stay in South Africa from 1893 to 1914 when he founded the Natal Indian Congress in 1894. It had an important influence on him and his ideas about the British Empire in India. How are these two (his experiences in South Africa and India) interconnected?

Mahatma Gandhi

6 The Freedom Charter – a constitution for the future?*

The Freedom Charter is an important document. It contains all the demands and aims the people opposing apartheid had in the 1950s. In order to collect the views of and represent all South Africans, the entire population of South Africa was asked to hand in their wishes and demands for inclusion in such a charter. It was seen as a future constitution for a unified South Africa. The Freedom Charter was adopted at the Congress of the People in Kliptown (near Johannesburg) on 26 Juni 1955. The Congress of People was made up of many organisations opposing apartheid and was attended by 3000 delegates including 320 Indians, 230 coloureds and 112 whites. – www.sahistory.org.za/pages/governence-projects/freedom-charter/07_charter.htm.

We, the People of South Africa,
declare for all our country and the world to know:

that South Africa belongs to all who live in it, black and white, and that no government can justly claim authority unless it is based on the will of all the people;
that our people have been robbed of their birthright to land, liberty and peace by a form of government founded on injustice and inequality;
that our country will never be prosperous or free until all our people live in brotherhood, enjoying equal rights and opportunities;
that only a democratic state, based on the will of all the people, can secure to all their birthright without distinction of colour, race, sex or belief;
And therefore, we, the people of South Africa, black and white together equals, countrymen and brothers adopt this Freedom Charter;
And we pledge ourselves to strive together, sparing neither strength nor courage, until the democratic changes here set out have been won.

The People Shall Govern!
Every man and woman shall have the right to vote for and to stand as a candidate for all bodies which make laws; [...]
The rights of the people shall be the same, regardless of race, colour or sex [...]

All National Groups Shall Have Equal Rights!
There shall be equal status in the bodies of state, in the courts and in the schools for all national groups and races;
All people shall have equal right to use their own languages, and to develop their own folk culture and customs;
All national groups shall be protected by law against insults to their race and national pride;
The preaching and practice of national, race or colour discrimination and contempt shall be a punishable crime;
All apartheid laws and practices shall be set aside.

The People Shall Share in the Country's Wealth!
The national wealth of our country, the heritage of South Africans, shall be restored to the people;
The mineral wealth beneath the soil, the Banks and monopoly industry shall be transferred to the ownership of the people as a whole;
All other industry and trade shall be controlled to assist the wellbeing of the people;
All people shall have equal rights to trade where they choose, to manufacture and to enter all trades, crafts and professions. [...]

All Shall be Equal Before the Law!
No-one shall be imprisoned, deported or restricted without a fair trial; No-one shall be condemned by the order of any Government official;
The courts shall be representative of all the people;
Imprisonment shall be only for serious crimes against the people, and shall aim at re-education, not vengeance;
The police force and army shall be open to all on an equal basis and shall be the helpers and protectors of the people;
All laws which discriminate on grounds of race, colour or belief shall be repealed.

All Shall Enjoy Equal Human Rights!
The law shall guarantee to all their right to speak, to organise, to meet together, to publish, to preach, to worship and to educate their children;
The privacy of the house from police raids shall be protected by law;
All shall be free to travel without restriction from countryside to town, from province to province, and from South Africa abroad;
Pass Laws, permits and all other laws restricting these freedoms shall be abolished. [...]

The Doors of Learning and Culture Shall be Opened!
The government shall discover, develop and encourage national talent for the enhancement of our cultural life;
All the cultural treasures of mankind shall be open to all, by free exchange of books, ideas and contact with other lands;
The aim of education shall be to teach the youth to love their people and their culture, to honour human brotherhood, liberty and peace;
Education shall be free, compulsory, universal and equal for all children; Higher education and technical

training shall be opened to all by means of state allowances and scholarships awarded on the basis of merit;

Adult illiteracy shall be ended by a mass state education plan;

Teachers shall have all the rights of other citizens;

The colour bar in cultural life, in sport and in education shall be abolished. [...]

There Shall be Peace and Friendship!

South Africa shall be a fully independent state which respects the rights and sovereignty of all nations;

South Africa shall strive to maintain world peace and the settlement of all international disputes by negotiation – not war;

Peace and friendship amongst all our people shall be secured by upholding the equal rights, opportunities and status of all;

The people of the protectorates Basutoland, Bechuanaland and Swaziland shall be free to decide for themselves their own future;

The right of all peoples of Africa to independence and self-government shall be recognised, and shall be the basis of close co-operation.

Let all people who love their people and their country now say, as we say here:

THESE FREEDOMS WE WILL FIGHT FOR, SIDE BY SIDE, THROUGHOUT OUR LIVES, UNTIL WE HAVE WON OUR LIBERTY

A speaker at the Congress of the People in Kliptown, Johannesburg (1955)

Vocabulary

7 prosperous (adj.): successful and rich - **13 pledge** (n.): to make s.o. give a firm promise - **13 to strive** (v.): to make a great effort to achieve s.th. - **35 heritage** (n.): important qualities, customs, and traditions that have been in a society for a long time - **43 to manufacture** (v.): to make or produce large qualities of goods to be sold, using machinery - **52 vengeance** (n.): s.th. violent or harmful that you do to s.o. in order to punish them for harming you, your family etc - **57 to repeal** (v.): if a government repeals a law it officially ends that law - **68 to abolish** (v.): to officially end a law, system etc, esp. one that has existed for a long time - **72 to enhance** (v.): to improve s.th. - **80 compulsory** (adj.): s.th. that is compulsory must be done because it is the law or because s.o. in authority orders you to - **84 merit** (n.): a good quality that makes s.th. deserve praise or admiration - **85 illiteracy** (n.): s.o. who is illiterate has not learned to read or write

Explanations

67 pass laws: legislation to control the movement of black South Africans. Passes/reference books included besides personal data an employer's signature which had to be renewed each month, authorisation to be in a particular area, and tax certificates. The laws were abolished in 1986. - **99 protectorate**: a territory of one state that is "protected" by another more powerful one; the state keeps its autonomy but is bound by certain obligations to the protecting state.

Awareness

1 What do you consider to be important basic human rights?

Comprehension

2 In some sentences every word begins with a capital letter. What reasons can you find for this?
3 Look at the structure of the charter. What are the key demands?

Analysis

4 Which areas of someone's life are referred to? Why?
5 What would be the ultimate aim of the charter?

Opinion

6 Which demands of the Freedom Charter were most important? Give reasons for your opinion.
7 The apartheid government considered the Freedom Charter to be a "Communist document". Find reasons for this opinion.

Project

8 Find out about the restrictive legislation of the apartheid regime that was established in the 1950s. Have a look at the main laws that were passed during this time. Which areas of life were affected by it?
9 Divide the class into groups of 3-5 students. Each group should find at least three laws and discuss them in class. What did they mean for ordinary people? To what extent were these laws an essential part of the segregation process?

7

James Matthews

"The Park"

James Matthews (*1929) is a writer of fiction and a journalist. His short story "The Park", which was first published in the quarterly magazine *Présence Africaine* in 1962, shows the effects of apartheid from the perspective of an African boy who passes a playground on his way from home to the white customers of his mother, who washes their clothes. – Jean Marquard (ed.): *A Century of South African Short Stories* (Craighall/RSA: A.D. Donker, 1986), pp. 317f., 323-326.

A picture from old apartheid times

He looked longingly at the children on the other side of the railings; the children sliding down the chute, landing with feet astride on the bouncy lawn; screaming as they almost touched the sky with each upward curve of their swings; their joyful demented shrieks at each dip of the merry-go-round. He looked at them and his body trembled and ached to share their joy; buttocks to fit board, and hands and feet to touch steel. Next to him, on the ground, was a bundle of clothing, washed and ironed, wrapped in a sheet.

Five small boys, pursued by two bigger ones, ran past, ignoring him. One of the bigger boys stopped. "What are you looking at, you brown ape?" the boy said, stooping to pick up a lump of clay. He recognized him. The boy had been present the day he was put out of the park. The boy pitched the lump, shattering it on the rail above his head, and the fragments fell on his face. [...]

As he walked he recalled his last visit to the park. Without hesitation he had gone through the gates and got onto the nearest swing. Even now he could feel that pleasurable thrill that travelled the length of his body as he rocketed himself higher, higher, until he felt that the swing would up-end him when it reached its peak. Almost leisurely he had allowed it to come to a halt like a pendulum shortening its stroke and then ran towards the see-saw. A white boy, about his own age, was seated opposite him. Accordionlike their legs folded to send the see saw jerking from the indentation it pounded in the grass. A hand pressed on his shoulder stopping a jerk. He turned around to look into the face of the attendant.

"Get off!"

Typical apartheid notice board

The skin tightened between his eyes. Why must I get off? What have I done? He held on, hands clamped onto the iron attached to the wooden see-saw. The white boy jumped off from the other end and stood a detached spectator.

"You must get off!" The attendant spoke in a low voice so that it would not carry to the people who were gathering. "The council say," he continued, "that us blacks don't use the same swings as the whites. You must use the swings where you stay," his voice apologizing for the uniform he wore that gave him the right to watch that little white boys and girls were not hurt while playing.

"There no park where I stay." He waved a hand in the direction of a block of flats. "Park on the other side of town but I don't know where." He walked past them. The mothers with their babies, pink and belching, cradled in their arms, the children lolling on the grass, his companion from the see-saw, the nurse girls – their uniforms their badge of indemnity – pushing prams. Beside him walked the attendant.

The attendant pointed an accusing finger at a notice board at the entrance. "There. You can read for yourself." Absolving him of all blame.

He struggled with the red letters on the white background. "Blankes Alleen. Whites Only." He walked through the gates and behind him the swings screeched, the see-saw rattled, and the merry-go-round rumbled. [...]

A thought came to his mind almost at the end of the meal. He sat spoon poised in the air shaken by its magnitude. Why not go to the park after dark? After it had closed its gates on the old men, the children, and nurses with their prams! There would be no one to stop him.

He could think no further. He was lightheaded with the thought of it. His mother's voice, as she related her day to his father, was not the steam that stung, but a soft breeze wafting past him, leaving him undisturbed. Then qualms troubled him. He had never been in that part of town at night. A band of fear tightened across his chest, contracting his insides, making it hard for him to swallow his food. He gripped his spoon tightly, stretching his skin across his knuckles.

I'll do it! I'll go to the park as soon as we're finished eating. He controlled himself with difficulty. He swallowed what was left on his plate and furtively watched to see how the others were faring. Hurry up! Hurry up! [...]

In front of him was the park with its gate and iron railings. Behind the railings, impaled, the notice board. He could see the swings beyond. The sight strengthened him.

He walked over, his breath coming faster. There was no one in sight. A car turned a corner and came towards him and he started at the sound of its engine. The car swept past, the tyres softly licking the asphalt.

The railings were icy-cold to his touch and the shock sent him into action. He extended his arms and with monkey-like movements pulled himself up to perch on top of the railings then dropped onto the newly turned earth.

The grass was damp with dew and he swept his feet across it. Then he ran and the wet grass bowed beneath his bare feet.

He ran towards the swings, the merry-go-round, see-saw to chute, hands covering the metal.

Up the steps to the top of the chute. He stood outlined against the sky. He was a bird; an eagle. He flung himself down on his stomach, sliding swiftly. Wheeeeeee! He rolled over when he slammed onto the grass. He looked at the moon for an instant then propelled himself to his feet and ran for the steps of the chute to recapture that feeling of flight. Each time he swept down the chute, he wanted the trip never to end, to go on sliding, sliding, sliding. [...]

Feet astride, hands clutching silver chains, he jerked his body to gain momentum. He crouched like a runner then violently straightened. The swing widened its arc. It swept higher, higher, higher. It reached the sky. He could touch the moon. He plucked a star to pin to his breast. The earth was far below. No bird could fly as high as he. Upwards and onwards he went.

A light switched on in the hut at the far side of the park. It was a small patch of yellow on a dark square. The door opened and he saw a figure in the doorway. Then the door was shut and the figure strode towards him. He knew it was the attendant. A torch glinted brightly as it swung at his side.

He continued swinging.

The attendant came to a halt in front of him, out of reach of the swing's arc, and flashed his torch. The light caught him in mid-air.

"God dammit!" the attendant swore. "I told you before you can't get on the swings."

The rattle of the chains when the boy shifted his feet was the only answer he received.

"Why you come back?"

"The swings. I come back for the swings."

The attendant catalogued the things denied them because of their colour. Even his job depended on their goodwill.

"Blerry whites! They get everything!" All his feelings urged him to leave the boy alone, to let him continue to enjoy himself but the fear that someone might see them hardened him.

"Get off! Go home!" he screamed, his voice harsh, his anger directed at the system that drove him against his own. "If you don't get off, I go for the police. You know what they do to you."

The swing raced back and forth.

The attendant turned and hurried towards the gate.

"Mama. Mama." His lips trembled, wishing himself safe in his mother's kitchen, sitting next to the still-burning stove with a comic spread across his knees. "Mama. Mama." His voice mounted, wrenched from this throat, keeping pace with the soaring swing as it climbed the sky. Voice and swing. Swing and voice. Higher. Higher. Higher. Until they were one.

At the entrance of the park the notice board stood tall, its shadow elongated, pointing towards him.

Vocabulary

4 chute (n.): a long narrow structure that slopes down - **10 demented** (adj.): behaving as if you are crazy - **18 to stoop** (v.): to bend your body forwards and down - **33 to up-end** (v.): to turn s.th. over so that it is standing upside down - **34 peak** (n.): the highest level, rate etc of s.th. - **36 see-saw** (n.): a piece of equipment that children play on, made of a board that is balanced in the middle - **39 indentation** (n.): a cut into the surface or edge of s.th. - **39 to pound** (v.): to hit s.th. many times with a tool in order to break it into pieces or make it flat - **40 jerk** (v.): to pull s.th. suddenly or roughly - **62 indemnity** (n.): protection against loss or damage - **82 qualm** (n.): a feeling/ slight worry because you are not sure that what you are doing is right - **89 furtive** (adj.): behaving as if you want to keep s.th. secret - **158 to wrench** (v.): to twist and pull s.th. from its position using force - **163 elongated** (adj.): longer than normal

Explanation

145 blerry: (South African English) euphemistic for bloody

James Matthews was born into a working class family in District Six (Cape Town) in 1929. He worked as a newspaper-seller, messenger and journalist. He published a volume of poetry, *Cry Rage* (1972), that was banned in South Africa. He was detained by the apartheid government in 1976. Matthews was a leading figure in the propagation of the ideas of the Black Consciousness Movement. He also published short story collections, among them *The Park and Other Stories* (1983). His novel *The Party is Over* was published after apartheid in 1997. He still lives on the Cape Flats (a township area around Cape Town).

Awareness

1 Why does the boy want to play in the park?

Comprehension

2 Why is the boy not allowed to play in the park?

3 How do the white boys behave towards the black boy?

4 What are the reasons for the behaviour of the attendant?

Analysis

5 Look at ll. 110 - 118 ("Up the steps [...] sliding, sliding, sliding.").
What does the boy achieve in that brief moment?

6 The boy does not have a name. Can you think of reasons for that?

7 Analyse l. 62. What is meant by a badge of indemnity?

Opinion

8 To what extent does the story represent the effects of apartheid on the life of the boy? Give reasons for your opinion.

Project

9 Read the entire short story. The boy's mother works as a washerwoman for white people. How is the relationship between whites and blacks characterised in the story? Which privileges are enjoyed by the whites in the story? How is the life of the black boy and his family portrayed?

8 The Sharpeville Massacre*

The Sharpeville Massacre in the 1960s was a turning point in South African history. For the resistance movements it marked the change from non-violent to violent protest. The peaceful protest at Sharpeville against the pass laws was organised by the Pan Africanist Congress (PAC) and met by shooting by the police. It is not clear what really happened on 21 March 1960; there were different versions of and perspectives on the events in Sharpeville. In the following text Humphrey Tyler, assistant editor of *Drum Magazine* at that time, reports how he experienced that day in his function as a journalist. – www.sahistory.org.za/pages/governence-projects/sharpeville/03_eyewitnesses.htm.

69 people were killed by the police during the Sharpeville Massacre

We went into Sharpeville the back way, behind a grey police car and three Saracens. As we drove through the fringes of the township many people shouted the Pan-Africanist slogan "Izwe Lethu", which means "Our Land", or gave the thumbs-up "freedom" salute and shouted "Afrika!". They were grinning, cheerful, and nobody seemed to be afraid…There were crowds in the streets as we approached the police station. There were plenty of police, too, wearing more guns and ammunition than uniforms…An African approached…and said he was the local Pan-Africanist leader. He told [us] his organisation was against violence and that the crowd was there for a peaceful demonstration…The crowd seemed perfectly amiable. It certainly never crossed our minds that they would attack us or anybody…

There were sudden shrill cries of "Izwe Lethu" - women's voices it sounded – from near the police, and I could see a small section of the crowd swirl around the Saracens and hands went up in the Africanist salute. Then the shooting started. We heard the chatter of a machine gun, then another, then another. There were hundreds of women, some of them laughing. They must have thought the police were firing blanks. One woman was hit about ten yards from our car. Her companion, a young man, went back when she fell. He thought she had stumbled. Then he turned her over and saw that her chest had been shot away. He looked at the blood on his hand and said: "My God, she's gone!" Hundreds of kids were running, too.

One little boy had on an old blanket coat, which he held up behind his head, thinking, perhaps, that it might save him from the bullets. Some of the children, hardly as tall as the grass, were leaping like rabbits. Some were shot, too. Still the shooting went on. One of the policemen was standing on top of a Saracen, and it looked as though he was firing his gun into the crowd. He was swinging it around in a wide arc from his hip as though he were panning a movie camera. Two other officers were with him, and it looked as if they were firing pistols. Most of the bodies were strewn on the road running through the field in which we were. One man, who had been lying still, dazedly got to his feet, staggered a few yards, then fell in a heap. A woman sat with her head cupped in her hands.

One by one the guns stopped.

Before the shooting, I heard no warning to the crowd to disperse. There was no warning volley. When the shooting started it did not stop until there was no living thing in the huge compound in front of the police station. The police have claimed they were in desperate danger because the crowd was stoning them. Yet only three policemen were reported to have been hit by stones – and more than 200 Africans were shot down. The police also have said that the crowd was armed with "ferocious weapons", which littered the compound after they fled.

I saw no weapons, although I looked very carefully, and afterwards studied the photographs of the death scene. While I was there I saw only shoes, hats and a few bicycles left among the bodies. The crowd gave me no reason to feel scared, though I moved among them without any distinguishing mark to protect me, quite obvious with my white skin. I think the police were scared though, and I think the crowd knew it.

The police used saracens to suppress riots

Vocabulary

3 fringe (n.): the part of s.th. that is farthest from the centre - **14 amiable** (adj.): friendly and likable - **18 to swirl** (v): to turn around quickly in a twisting circular movement or make s.th. do this - **26 blank** (n.): a cartridge that contains an explosive but not a bullet - **48 to pan** (v.): if a film or television camera pans in a particular direction, it moves and follows the thing that is being filmed - **52 dazed** (adj.): unable to think clearly, esp. because of a shock, accident etc - **57 to disperse** (v.): if a group of people disperses or is dispersed, they separate and go away in different directions - **57 volley** (n.): a large number of shots fired from a gun at the same time - **65 ferocious** (adj.): violent, dangerous, and frightening

Explanations

Introduction: **pass laws**: see p. 20 - **Introduction**: **PAC**: Pan Africanist Congress of Azania; it was a resistance movement established in 1959 and the major rival of the ANC (see p. 17). The PAC proclaimed Africanism and opposed multi-racialism; their key slogan in the past was "Africa for the Africans" - **Introduction**: ***Drum* magazine**: see p. 57 - **2 saracens**: armoured cars that were often used to suppress riots in the townships (see p. 28)

Awareness

1 What is meant by a turning point in history?
2 Can you find such turning points in German history?

Comprehension

3 What was the atmosphere in the crowd like at the beginning of the demonstration?
4 Why did the situation change?

Analysis

5 Compare the eye-witness account of Humphrey Tyler with an article in the British newspaper *The Guardian* (http://www.guardian.co.uk/world/1960/mar/22/southafrica.fromthearchive). The differences are significant. Try to find reasons for this. Can you find any similarities in the two accounts?

Opinion

6 What do you believe happened in Sharpeville in March 1960? Give reasons for your opinion.
7 To what extent can reporting on certain events be objective or neutral? What are the implications for journalists and the readers of such reports?

Project

8 In groups of 4-5 students write an article about a recent event, but from different perspectives. Compare your articles. To what extent do they differ from each other? How could they be used to manipulate public opinion?

9

Nelson Mandela

"I am prepared to die"*

Nelson Mandela, prominent leader of the ANC (African National Congress) and founder of the ANC's military wing "Umkhonto we Sizwe (MK)", was declared a terrorist by the apartheid regime and charged with sabotage in the so-called Rivonia Trial (1963-64). An impending death penalty was converted to lifelong imprisonment on notorious Robben Island, off the shores of Cape Town. The statement which he prepared for the opening of the defence case in the Rivonia Trial in Pretoria Supreme Court on 20 April 1964 is a powerful and courageous speech that reflects on the importance of resistance against the racist system. – www.anc.org.za/show.php?doc=ancdocs/history/mandela/1960s/rivonia.html.

A shack in the Transkei

[...] At the outset, I want to say that the suggestion made by the State in its opening that the struggle in South Africa is under the influence of foreigners or communists is wholly incorrect. I have done whatever I did, both as an individual and as a leader of my people, because of my experience in South Africa and my own proudly felt African background, and not because of what any outsider might have said.

In my youth in the Transkei I listened to the elders of my tribe telling stories of the old days. Amongst the tales they related to me were those of wars fought by our ancestors in defence of the fatherland. The names of Dingane and Bambata, Hintsa and Makana, Squngthi and Dalasile, Moshoeshoe and Sekhukhuni, were praised as the glory of the entire African nation. I hoped then that life might offer me the opportunity to serve my people and make my own humble contribution to their freedom struggle. This is what has motivated me in all that I have done in relation to the charges made against me in this case. [...]

South Africa is the richest country in Africa, and could be one of the richest countries in the world. But it is a land of extremes and remarkable contrasts. The whites enjoy what may well be the highest standard of living in the world, whilst Africans live in poverty and misery. Forty per cent of the Africans live in hopelessly overcrowded and, in some cases, drought-stricken Reserves, where soil erosion and the overworking of the soil makes it impossible for them to live properly off the land. Thirty per cent are labourers, labour tenants, and squatters on white farms and work and live under conditions similar to those of the serfs of the Middle Ages. The other 30 per cent live in towns where they have developed economic and social habits which bring them closer in many respects to white standards. Yet most Africans, even in this group, are impoverished by low incomes and high cost of living. [...]

The complaint of Africans, however, is not only that they are poor and the whites are rich, but that the laws which are made by the whites are designed to preserve this situation. There are two ways to break out of poverty. The first is by formal education, and the second is by the worker acquiring a greater skill at his work and thus higher wages. As far as Africans are concerned, both these avenues of advancement are deliberately curtailed by legislation. [...]

There is compulsory education for all white children at virtually no cost to their parents, be they rich or poor. Similar facilities are not provided for the African children, though there are some who receive such assistance. African children, however, generally have to pay more for their schooling than whites. According to figures quoted by the South African Institute of Race Relations in its 1963 journal, approximately 40 per cent of African children in the age group between seven to fourteen do not attend school. For those who do attend school, the standards are vastly different from those afforded to white children. [...]

The other main obstacle to the economic advancement of the African is the industrial colour-bar under which all the better jobs of industry are reserved for Whites only. [...] Strikes of African workers are illegal, and [...] they are denied the right of collective bargaining which is permitted to the better-paid White workers. [...]

The lack of human dignity experienced by Africans is the direct result of the policy of white supremacy. White supremacy implies black inferiority. Legislation designed to preserve white supremacy entrenches this notion. Menial tasks in South Africa are invariably performed by Africans. [...] Because of this sort of attitude, whites tend to regard Africans as a separate breed. They do not look upon them as people with families of their own; they do not realize that they have emotions - that they fall in love like white people do; that they want to be with their wives and children like white people want to be with theirs; that they want to earn enough money to support their families properly, to feed and clothe them and send them to school. And what "house-boy" or "garden-boy" or labourer can ever hope to do this?

Pass laws, which to the Africans are among the most hated bits of legislation in South Africa, render any African liable to police surveillance at any time. [...] Hundreds and thousands of Africans are thrown into jail each year under pass laws. Even worse than this is the fact that pass laws keep husband and wife apart and lead to the breakdown of family life.

Poverty and the breakdown of family life have secondary effects. Children wander about the streets of the townships because they have no schools to go to, or no money to enable them to go to school, or no parents at home to see that they go to school, because both parents (if there be two) have to work to keep the family alive. This leads to a breakdown in moral standards, to an alarming rise in illegitimacy, and to growing violence which erupts not only politically, but everywhere. Life in the townships is dangerous. There is not a day that goes by without somebody being stabbed or assaulted. And violence is carried out of the townships in the white living areas. People are afraid to walk alone in the streets after dark. Housebreakings and robberies are increasing, despite the fact that the death sentence can now be imposed for such offences. Death sentences cannot cure the festering sore. Africans want to be paid a living wage. Africans want to perform work which they are capable of doing, and not work which the Government declares them to be capable of. Africans want to be allowed to live where they obtain work, and not be endorsed out of an area because they were not born there. Africans want to be allowed to own land in places where they work, and not to be obliged to live in rented houses which they can never call their own. Africans want to be part of the general population, and not confined to living in their own ghettoes. African men want to have their wives and children to live with them where they work, and not be forced into an unnatural existence in men's hostels. African women want to be with their menfolk and not be left permanently widowed in the Reserves. Africans want to be allowed out after eleven o'clock at night and not to be confined to their rooms like little children. Africans want to be allowed to travel in their own country and to seek work where they want to and not where the Labour Bureau tells them to. Africans want a just share in the whole of South Africa; they want security and a stake in society.

Above all, we want equal political rights, because without them our disabilities will be permanent. I know this sounds revolutionary to the whites in this country, because the majority of voters will be Africans. This makes the white man fear democracy.

But this fear cannot be allowed to stand in the way of the only solution which will guarantee racial harmony and freedom for all. It is not true that the enfranchisement of all will result in racial domination. Political division, based on colour, is entirely artificial and, when it disappears, so will the domination of one colour group by another. The ANC has spent half a century fighting against racialism. When it triumphs it will not change that policy.

This then is what the ANC is fighting. Their struggle is a truly national one. It is a struggle of the African people, inspired by their own suffering and their own experience. It is a struggle for the right to live.

During my lifetime I have dedicated myself to this struggle of the African people. I have fought against white domination, and I have fought against black domination. I have cherished the ideal of a democratic and free society in which all persons live together in harmony and with equal opportunities. It is an ideal which I hope to live for and to achieve. But if needs be, it is an ideal for which I am prepared to die.

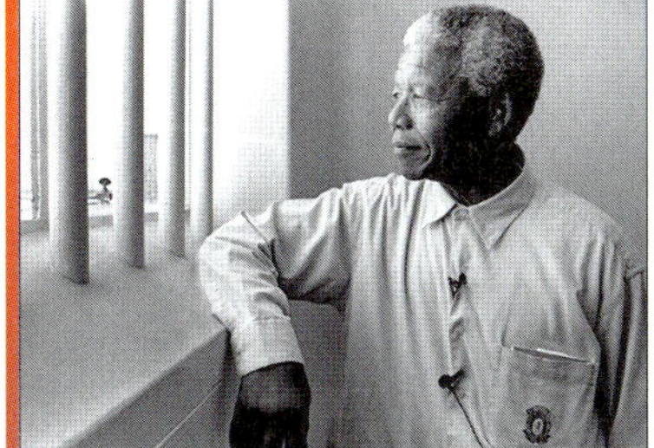

Nelson Mandela – Icon of the Rainbow Nation

In 2008 Nelson Rolihlahla Mandela celebrated his 90th birthday. He was born in a little village called Qunu in the Transkei in 1918. During the 1950s he was involved in ANC politics and soon became a leading figure in the resistance movement. In the so-called Rivonia Trial he was sentenced to life imprisonment on Robben Island. Nelson Mandela stayed in prison for 27 years and became the symbol of South African resistance against apartheid. Before and after his release from prison on 11 February 1990, he negotiated a free and democratic South Africa with the apartheid government. He was inaugurated as the country's first black president after the first free elections in April 1994. He is one of the most impressive and influential politicians of the 20th and 21st centuries. His way of dealing with all members of South African society including the former oppressors as well as his prison wardens is remarkable and characterised by forgiveness and understanding.

The sculptures of Nobel Prize winners Albert Luthuli, Desmond Tutu, F. W. de Klerk and Nelson Mandela in Nobel Square, Cape Town

Vocabulary

Introduction: **to be charged with** (v.): to state officially that s.o. is guilty of a crime - **Introduction**: **impending** (adj.): an impending event or situation is going to happen very soon - **Introduction**: **notorious** (adj.): famous or well-known for s.th. bad - **1 outset** (n.): at or from the beginning of an event or process - **12 ancestor** (n.): a member of your family who lived a long time ago - **17 humble** (adj.): not considering yourself or your ideas as important as other people's - **27 drought-stricken** (adj.): very badly affected by a long period of dry weather when there is not enough water for plants and animals to live - **29 to live off** (phr. v.): to get your income or food from a supply of money or from another person - **31 squatter** (n.): s.o. who lives in an empty building or on a piece of land without permission and without paying rent - **32 serf** (n.): s.o. in former times who lived and worked on land that they did not own and who had to obey the owner of the land - **36 to impoverish** (v.): to make s.o. very poor - **43 to acquire** (v.): to learn or develop skills etc by your own efforts - **45 advancement** (n.): progress or development in your job, level of knowledge - **45 to curtail** (v.): to reduce s.th. such as the amount of money you spend - **47 compulsory** (adj.): s.th. that is compulsory must be done because it is the law or because s.o. in authority orders you to - **63 bargaining** (n.): discussion in order to reach agreement about a sale, contract etc - **66 dignity** (n.): a calm and serious manner or quality - **69 entrenched** (adj.): strongly established and not likely to change - **83 to render s.o. liable** (phr. v.): to make s.o. legally responsible - **84 surveillance** (n.): /sə'veɪləns||sər/ the act of carefully watching a person or place because they may be connected with criminal activities - **96 illegitimacy** (n.): /ˌɪl$^{ɪ}_{ə}$'dʒɪt$^{ɪ}_{ə}$m$^{ɪ}_{ə}$si/ born to parents who are not married - **104 to impose** (v.): to officially order that something should be forbidden, restricted, taxed etc, or that s.o. should be punished - **109 to obtain** (v.): to get s.th. that you want - **110 to endorse** (v.): to express formal support or approval for s.o. or s.th. - **126 stake** (n.): to have an important part or share - **134 enfranchisement** (n.): to give a group of people the right to vote - **145 to dedicate yourself to s.th.** (phr. v.): to decide to spend all your time on and put all your efforts into one particular thing

Explanations

Introduction: **Rivonia Trial**: trial of ten Umkhonto we Sizwe ("Spear of the nation"; military wing of the ANC) leaders in Pretoria between 1963-1964. They were charged with high treason (possible death sentence), but only found guilty of sabotage (life imprisonment). - **13 Dingane/Dingaan**: c.1795-1840, Zulu (see p. 5) king who assumed power in 1828. He killed the trekboer (cf. Chapter 3) leader Piet Retief and was then defeated in the Blood River battle in 1838 by the trekboers (Dutch-speaking farmers who migrated from the Cape Colony to the South African interior). He was murdered in Swaziland. - **13 Bambata**: c. 1865-1906, Zulu (see p. 5) sub-ruler. He and his followers were engaged in guerrilla resistance against the colonial authorities. He was killed in an ambush. - **13 Hintsa**: c. 1790-1835, paramount chief of the Xhosa (see p. 5) from 1804. He led the opposition against settlers in the Cape Colony (see p. 14) in the frontier wars (series of conflicts between the British and the Xhosa in the Eastern Cape region) of the 1830s. He was killed by the British. - **13 Makana/Makhanda**: Xhosa (see p. 5) warrior-prophet. He led an unsuccessful attack on Grahamstown in the frontier war of 1818-19. He surrendered in 1819 and was sent to Robben Island as a prisoner. - **13 Squngthi**: A lesser known African leader. No further information available. - **14 Dalasile**: Chief of the amaQwati tribe - **14 Moshoeshoe/Moshweshwe**: 1786-1870, first paramount chief of the Sotho (see p. 5) and founding father of Basutoland (state in the mountainous region of the Drakensberg). He was known for his diplomatic way of dealing with outside raiders, such as Sotho rivals, Nguni-speaking attackers and the trekboers (cf. Chapter 3). - **14 Sekhukhuni** (also called Masile): c. 1810-1882, paramount chief of the Bapedi (see p. 5) from 1861. He fought against the trekboers (cf. Chapter 3) and the British after they annexed the Transvaal (see p. 14). He was defeated in 1879 and imprisoned. He was released in 1881. - **28 Reserves**: small portions of land were set aside for various black groups by the colonial forces in the 19th century. They were used as reservoirs of labour. The reserves later were incorporated into the Bantustan/homelands policy of apartheid (transformation of the African reserves into self-governing states; they were led by appointed chiefs and headmen who were puppets of the apartheid regime; the Bantustans were dependent on South Africa). - **53 South African Institute of Race Relations (SAIRR)**: a non-governmental organisation established in 1929 and dedicated to the research of race relations. It found itself in opposition to the interests of the apartheid regime. - **60 industrial colour-bar**: colour bar is another word for job reservation. Certain jobs were reserved for whites only, thus restricting the job opportunities of all other ethnic groups in South Africa. - **82 pass laws**: see p. 20 - **91 townships**: they were built on the outskirts of urban areas. Africans, Indians and coloureds were restricted to these areas. They were also segregated according to "race". As townships were semi-illegal, they were often raided, some even destroyed, by the police. The most famous one is Soweto (an abbreviation of South Western Townships), now part of Johannesburg. - **118 men's hostel**: living quarters for rural Africans who came to work in the cities. Women/wives were not allowed to live there. Hostels were known for being very small and overcrowded. There was no privacy at all because the men had to share the dormitory and the bathrooms. There were also no kitchen facilities.

Awareness

1 Can you imagine what a homeland is? What do you know about the homelands in South Africa during apartheid?

Comprehension

2 How is South Africa described in Mandela's statement?
3 Why does Mandela make a distinction between outsiders and South Africa itself at the beginning of his statement (see ll. 1 - 8)?
4 According to Mandela, what are the secondary effects of apartheid?
5 What did the ANC and Mandela demand for Africans (see p. 5)?

Analysis

6 Right from the beginning of the statement Mandela talks about the individual and the community. What does that mean and why is it important for him?
7 Look at the language used in the speech. Analyse the literary devices that you can find. What is their function?

Opinion

8 Why does Mandela mention African leaders?
9 Why does Mandela refer to the feelings of Africans?

Project

10 Nelson Mandela is a prominent figure in the struggle for liberation and in today's South Africa. He is a living legend. Find out more about his extraordinary personality. Why is he seen as one of the most influential political leaders of the 20th and 21st century?

10

Steve Biko

"The definition of Black Consciousness"

Steve Biko was a leading figure of the Black Consciousness Movement (BCM) which adopted a pro-black doctrine. The aim of the BCM was to re-evaluate black identities and to instil pride in their African heritage and traditions. This ideology had a great impact on the Soweto Uprising. Steve Biko defines the term "Black Consciousness" and talks about the aims of this ideology in his paper "The Definition of Black Consciousness" (1971). - Aelred Stubbs, C. R. (ed.): *I Write What I Like* (London: Heinemann 1984), pp. 48f., 52f.

We have in our policy manifesto defined blacks as those who are by law or tradition politically, economically and socially discriminated against as a group in the South African society and identifying themselves as a unit in the struggle towards the realisation of their aspirations. This definition illustrates to us a number of things:

1. Being black is not a matter of pigmentation – being black is a reflection of a mental attitude.

2. Merely by describing yourself as black you have started on a road towards emancipation, you have committed yourself to fight against all forces that seek to use your blackness as a stamp that marks you out as a subservient being. [...]

Briefly defined therefore, Black Consciousness is in essence the realisation by the black man of the need to rally together with his brothers around the cause of their operation – the blackness of their skin – and to operate as a group in order to rid themselves of the shackles that bind them to perpetual servitude. It seeks to demonstrate the lie that black is an aberration from the "normal" which is white. It is a manifestation of a new realisation that by seeking to run away from themselves and to emulate the white man, blacks are insulting the intelligence of whoever created them black. Black Consciousness therefore, takes cognizance of the deliberateness of God's plan in creating black people black. It seeks to infuse the black community with a new-found pride in themselves, their efforts, their value systems, their culture, their religion and their outlook to life. [...]

Blacks are out to completely transform the system and to make of it what they wish. Such a major undertaking can only be realised in an atmosphere where people are convinced of the truth inherent in their stand. Liberation therefore, is of paramount importance in the concept of Black Consciousness, for we cannot be conscious of ourselves and yet remain in bondage. We want to attain the envisioned self which is a free self. [...]

The importance of black solidarity to the various segments of the black community must not be understated. There have been in the past a lot of suggestions that there can be no viable unity amongst blacks because they hold each other in contempt. Coloureds despise Africans because they, (the former) by their proximity to the Africans, may lose the chances of assimilation into the white world. Africans despise the Coloureds and Indians for a variety of reasons. Indians not only despise Africans but in many instances also exploit the Africans in job and shop situations. All these stereotype attitudes have led to mountainous inter-group suspicions amongst the blacks.

What we should at all times look at is the fact that:

1. We are all oppressed by the same system.

2. That we are oppressed to varying degrees is a deliberate design to stratify us not only socially but also in terms of aspirations.

3. Therefore it is to be expected that in terms of the enemy's plan there must be this suspicion and that if we are committed to the problem of emancipation to the same degree it is part of our duty to bring to the attention of the black people the deliberateness of the enemy's subjugation scheme.

4. That we should go on with our programme, attracting to it only committed people and not just those eager to see an equitable distribution of groups amongst our ranks. This is a game common amongst liberals. The one criterion that must govern all our action is commitment.

Further implications of Black Consciousness are to do with correcting false images of ourselves in terms of Culture, Education, Religion, Economics. The importance of this also must not be understated. There is always an interplay between the history of a people i.e. the past, and their faith in themselves and hopes for their future. We are aware of the terrible role played by our education and religion in creating amongst us a false understanding of ourselves. We must therefore work out schemes not only to correct this, but further to be our own authorities rather than wait to be interpreted by others. Whites can only see us from the outside and as such can never extract and analyse the ethos in the black community.

Stephen Bantu Biko was born in King William's Town (Eastern Cape) in 1946. He was a student leader and founder of the South African Student Organisation (SASO). He promoted self-reliance among black people and became the chief ideologist for the Black Consciousness Movement. Although Steve Biko did not actively participate in the Soweto Uprising of 1976, the ideas of the Black Consciousness Movement formed the backdrop to this important event. Steve Biko was detained in 1977 and died in police custody on 12 September of the same year as a result of the brain damage that he suffered through severe torture in detention.

Vocabulary

5 aspiration (n.): a strong desire to have or achieve s.th. - **13 subservient** (adj.): s.o. who is subservient is too willing to do what other people want them to do - **18 shackle** (n.): *literary* the limits put on your freedom and happiness by slavery etc - **19 perpetual** (adj.): continuing all the time without stopping - **19 servitude** (n.): the condition of being a slave or being forced to obey s.o. else - **20 aberration** (n.): an action or event that is different from what usually happens or what s.o. usually does - **23 to emulate** (v.): to try to be like s.o. else because you admire them - **25 cognizance** (n.): knowledge or understanding of s.th. - **27 to infuse** (v.): to fill s.th. or s.o. with a particular feeling or quality - **42 viable** (adj.): a viable plan or system can work successfully - **44 to despise** (v.): to dislike s.o. or s.th. very much - **55 stratified** (adj.): having different social classes - **62 subjugation** (n.): to defeat a person or group and make them obey you - **65 equitable** (adj.): an equitable action, process etc treats everyone in an equal way; fair

Explanations

Introduction: **Soweto Uprising**: see p. 33

Denzel Washington as Steve Biko in Cry Freedom *(1987)*

Awareness

1 Imagine what it was like to be a black South African in the 1960s. What would be your role in society? What would be your opportunities?

Comprehension

2 How is "blackness" defined?
3 What does Biko say about the relationship between racial groups?

Analysis

4 What are the aims of the BCM?
5 What are the implications of the BCM for the South African community?
6 Analyse ll. 7f. Would you agree with this sentence? What are its implications?
7 Compare Biko's paper and Mandela's speech at the Rivonia trial (text 9). What do the two documents have in common? To what extent do they differ from each other?

Opinion

8 Is an ideology like BCM necessary for a resistance movement?
9 Write your own comment on Steve Biko's statement about "the deliberateness of God's plan in creating black people black." (ll. 25-27)

Projects

10 The BCM is often compared to developments in the US in the 1960s. Find out about the civil rights movement in the USA. What were the aims of the American civil rights movement? What do the BCM and the American civil rights movement have in common?
11 Touched by Biko's fate, the musician and songwriter Peter Gabriel wrote a song called "Biko". Find the lyrics on the internet (http://www.azlyrics.com/lyrics/petergabriel/biko.html) or see the song performed (http://www.youtube.com/watch?v=wpk4kcMVOA0). Analyse the song paying special attention to the literary devices used. What do you think the song might intend to achieve?

Film Analysis

12 The film *Cry Freedom* (1987) by Sir Richard Attenborough focuses on Steve Biko and his friendship with the journalist Donald Woods. The film is based on Woods' biography of Biko. Watch the film. How does it represent the apartheid state?
13 How is Steve Biko portrayed? Why is he considered to be an enemy of the state? Why did he become a central figure in the struggle against apartheid?
14 What do you learn about the BCM in the film?

11

Dan Moyane

The Soweto Uprising and its aftermath*

Dan Moyane was a student at the Morris Isaacson High School in Soweto in the 1970s. He participated in the protests against Afrikaans (see p. 10). In an interview, he speaks about his experiences on that fateful day in June 1976. – Brink, Elsabé et al.: *Recollected 25 years later: SOWETO 16 June 1976* (Cape Town: Kwela Books 2001), pp. 59-62.

Dan: We were singing and it was jovial, the mood, exciting, and with the placards we started going, we started going. We went and went. We passed Mofolo, other people were joining us as we were going along, other kids, and everybody was in school uniform, everyone. You looked around from left to right, people were in their various school uniforms.

Question: Was there tension at that stage?

Dan: There was no tension. There was that anticipation, that sense of ... Wow! You know positively, what is going to happen? We were all going to Orlando Stadium, and there we will publicly endorse a memorandum that will then be delivered by our leaders, who had organised this, to the government, [saying] that we don't want to be taught in Afrikaans in school. Or at least we need to have a choice, because they were making it compulsory that we be taught in Afrikaans. We don't mind learning Afrikaans as a language, but it is against international convention. I mean, where else are you going to go with an Afrikaans degree? [...]

He said: "Listen, police are further down the road, they have closed [the road]. They say we don't have permission for the march and they won't allow us to pass. We told them we want to go and just hand in the memorandum at Orlando Stadium, the others are coming there and were going to meet." [...]

There's a street that was coming from the houses, the other kids were there coming from Orlando West, so it was just packed around the side streets, from the main streets. And then I don't know what happened, because I didn't see it. He came down, and then we were there, and people saying, 'Hey, hey, hey,' and then suddenly there was this gunshot.

This gunshot suddenly, and we were down. I was 600 metres from there and people were running from that road and they were coming that way and they were saying that the police are shooting at us, I don't know what happened, and we just picked up stones. And I've never seen so many stones coming. It was a huge crowd – those police could not stand there, they would have been killed. By then Hector had been shot, and the news filtered that there was a kid who had been shot. [...]

Question: Hector was thirteen. Was it a stray bullet or was it just an un-aimed shot?

Dan: I don't know if it was stray, because he was shot in one of the side streets, coming towards the main road. [I don't know] whether it was directed at him as a person or it was a bullet that these boers were shooting. I think there must have been a shot or two up, whatever, but the rest were shots into the crowd. The crowds were on the left, on the right and in the middle, and the stones came, and then the police retreated, they went, they ran further down. [...]

Then people were saying let's go back because the police are down there and then all hell broke loose. [...]

We all went backwards now, and then at the municipality [offices] at Mofolo, Dube, things just went out of control. That whole day the fire by the municipal offices started, and beer halls started, and then helicopters came. Tear-gas, I smelled tear-gas for the first time on that day.

Hector Petersen was one of the first victims

Info

Soweto Uprising

The Soweto Uprising, like the Sharpeville Massacre, is a turning point in South African history. On June 16, 1976 thousands of schoolchildren in Soweto protested against the government's plan to use Afrikaans as a medium of instruction. The police opened fire on the peaceful demonstration. One of the first victims was Hector Petersen, a thirteen-year-old boy (see photo). The protests spread throughout South Africa and were met by more violence. About 600 people were killed; thousands fled abroad and joined the liberation movements. The Soweto Uprising marks the beginning of the violent struggle against the apartheid regime. It also mirrors a younger generation that decided to take their destiny into their own hands. From this point onwards the violence and conflict between the government and the liberation movements increased and finally escalated into an internal civil war that would last until the beginning of the 1990s.

Vocabulary

1 jovial (adj.): friendly, cheerful - **9 anticipation** (n.): the act of expecting s.th. to happen - **12 to endorse** (v.): to express formal support or approval for s.o. or s.th. - **76 municipality** (n.): the government of a town, city etc, which makes decisions about local affairs

Explanations

Introduction: **Soweto**: one of the largest and best known townships in South Africa. Soweto stands for "South Western Township" - **3 ff. Mofolo, Orlando, Orlando West, Dube**: different parts of Soweto. Mofolo and Dube are in the middle of Soweto, while Orlando and Orlando West are in the northeastern direction. - **61 boer**: was used as a term to refer to Afrikaners (see p. 5); it is no longer used because it is derogatory.

The Peace and Democracy sculpture on Noble Square, A & V Waterfront, Cape Town

Awareness

1 Have you ever been to or taken part in a demonstration? How did you feel?

Comprehension

2 What happened after the first gunshots?
3 What kinds of weapons were used by the opposing sides?

Analysis

4 How is the atmosphere among the protesters described at the beginning of the text?
5 How did the crowd react to the shots?
6 What kind of language does Dan use in his account of the Soweto Uprising?

Opinion

7 Why did the students protest against using Afrikaans in schools?
8 What impression of the Soweto Uprising do you gain from Dan's account?

Project

9 Find out how the Soweto Uprising is remembered in South Africa today.
You could use the following websites: http://www.southafrica.info/about/history/hector-pieterson.htm, http://www.joburg.org.za/component/option,com_wrapper/Itemid,143/ and http://www.sahistory.org.za/pages/governence-projects/june16/index.htm.
Which measures were taken to keep the memory of the Soweto Uprising alive?

12 "Vote of the century opens era of hope"

After years of negotiations (1990-1994) between the main antagonists, the ANC (African National Congress) and the National Party (NP), and after many attempts to prevent these talks in various ways, the dates for the first free elections were finally settled: 26-29 April 1994. Nineteen parties appointed candidates for the elections and 86 % of the population (nearly 20 million people) went to the polling stations. It was a logistic challenge, but also a great success. Many people voted for the first time in their lives. The newspaper article published in the British newspaper *The Guardian* on 28 April 1994 by Gary Younge captures the atmosphere during the first free elections in South Africa. – www.guardian.co.uk/world/1994/apr/28/southafrica.garyyounge.

South Africans patiently queued in front of the polling stations in order to cast their votes

As dawn broke over Zone 9 of Meadowlands, Soweto, yesterday, the Mwale family was preparing for power.

First there was water to boil since the rumour had spread that the rightwing AWB might poison Meadowland's main tank. Esther Mwale said "most people with sense" in Zone 9 were boiling water.

Then, there was the huge pot of mealies – a staple of the township diet – to cook. On Tuesday, Granny had waited seven hours to cast her vote and they had had to bring her dinner while she queued. If there were long delays today, it would be her turn to come to the rescue.

Finally, there were the ID documents to find. No one could say the Mwales were not ready for democracy. As they set off at 7am, joining a human stream of hundreds on the main road, it seemed that all of Zone 9 had the same idea: first watch Nelson Mandela cast his vote in Durban on the television and then get down to the polling station at the Maponyane school quickly to beat the rush.

The clientele of Johannes' shebeen (township bar) had discussed this eventuality the night before. At the beginning of the evening, Jacob's solution to avoiding Tuesday's chaos was to get there early. A couple of hours and a few beers later, the prospect of waking up at 5am and queuing for two hours looked increasingly unattractive.

Mzimasi suggested going to vote in a white suburb, where the queues would be shorter, but nobody knew anyone with a car who could take them.

Johannes said he was voting ANC "for his children". But nobody else was prepared to say how they would vote. The talk was of logistics, not politics. Nevertheless, the sight of a white woman, who had cast her vote abroad, saying tearfully on television, "I'm just scared about the future", aroused some fierce emotion.

"What are you scared of? That a black man will run the country," shouted Mzimasi, slightly blowing his cover.

If Mzimasi was right about the woman's fears, the sight at Maponyane school yesterday morning would have confirmed them. Long queues of black people were waiting to have a say in their country's future. Many had dressed up for the occasion as if they were going to church. Men in suits, hats and clean shoes, women with fresh hair-does and wearing more make-up than is usually seen in the township.

After they had solved whatever problems they had had, people queued for about two hours before they could vote. While they waited, they joked, called to friends in other queues and scolded their bored children. Anything, in fact, but talk about politics.

After they had voted, nobody seemed to feel the urge to discuss the deeper significance of the day's events because nothing so obvious was necessary. There was just a keen sense of relief and confident smiles borne from the satisfaction at seeing a job well done. "It was easy. Just like they have been telling us on the television. I feel good now it's over," said Esther.

By the time the Mwales had finished voting, the queue was twice as long and Esther chided some of those at the back for being so lazy.

On the way home we saw Jacob, looking the worse for wear and being ribbed by friends at the bus stop. He had woken up late but was insisting he would still make it to the polling booths.

At the shebeen, Johannes had devised a plan to make sure Jacob kept his promise. No beer would be served to people without the white, fluorescent strip on their hand, which proved that they had voted. With a wry smile, he said: "How can there be a free and fair election if drunk people are going to vote?"

Nelson Mandela casting his vote during the first free election in South Africa

Vocabulary

Introduction: **polling** (n.): the activity of voting in a political election - **7 mealie** (n): (South African English) maize, or a piece of maize - **7 staple** (n.): a food that is needed and used all the time - **9 to cast a vote** (v.): to vote in an election - **57 to scold** (v.): to angrily criticise s.o., esp. a child, about s.th. they have done - **68 to chide** (v.): *literary* to speak angrily to s.o. because you do not approve of s.th. they have done - **72 to rib** (v.): *infml.* to make jokes and laugh at s.o. so that you embarrass them, but in a friendly way - **81 wry** (adj.): showing a mixture of amusement and displeasure or disbelief

Explanations

Introduction: **ANC**: see p. 17 - **4 AWB**: abbreviation for Afrikaner Weerstandsbeweging, a paramilitary right-wing organisation. It emerged in the late 1970s and is led by the notorious Eugene Terre'blanche. Their aim is an independent Afrikaner (see p. 5) volkstaat. - **20 Johannes**: owner of the shebeen - **20 shebeen**: a bar in a township where home brewed beer or liquor is often sold - **20 township**: see p. 28 - **22 Jacob, 29 Mzimasi**: customers in Johannes' shebeen

Info

Political parties in 1994

The most important and influential parties in South Africa in the 1990s were the African National Congress (ANC), the Pan Africanist Congress of Azania (PAC), the Inkatha Freedom Party (IFP), the Democratic Party (DP) and the National Party (NP), reflecting a wide range of political ideologies.

The ANC (see p. 17) and the PAC were rivals in the past. The PAC broke away from the ANC in 1958. The reasons for this were that the PAC favoured an exclusive black membership and followed an Africanist approach (their slogan was "Africa for the Africans"). The PAC launched the anti-pass law campaign in Sharpeville in 1960 (see p. 24 f.). Like the ANC it was banned by the apartheid government, its leaders went into exile and formed an armed wing, the Azanian People's Liberation Army (APLA). The ANC and the PAC were unbanned in 1990. The PAC refused to put down its weapons and continued its terrorist attacks on white civilians in the 1990s. In the elections of 1994 the PAC received only 1.8 % of the votes.

The IFP started out as a Zulu cultural organisation in 1922/23 and was revived by Mangosuthu Buthelezi in 1975. Buthelezi's approach was to work within the system of the homeland policy of the apartheid government. This was one reason why Inkatha broke with the ANC in 1979. In addition, it did not want to accept the authority of the ANC leadership in exile. The Inkatha became a political party in 1990. The struggle for power let to violent and bloody clashes between ANC supporters and members of Inkatha during the 1990s. In the elections the IFP gained 10.5% of the votes.

The Progressive Federal Party and liberals from the National Party (NP) merged to form the DP, a party left of the apartheid government, in 1989. Members of this party were involved in the negotiation process in the 1990s. In the 1994s election the DP won 1.7%.

The NP was founded in 1914. It was a conservative party and represented Afrikaner (see p. 5) interests. It became the leading political party from 1948 to 1990 and implemented apartheid in South Africa. Its voters consisted of Afrikaners and a growing number of English speaking South Africans. It was mainly responsible for the oppression of the black majority and the violent internal civil war unfolding in the 1970s and 1980s. F.W. de Klerk, an NP leader, released political prisoners and unbanned the opposition movements in 1990. The ANC and the NP negotiated the path to the first free elections and democracy in South Africa. The NP won 20% in the elections in 1994.

Awareness

1 What proportion of the population vote in your country?

Comprehension

2 What was the general atmosphere like at the polling station in the township?
3 Why did the shebeen owner Johannes only serve customers who already had been at the polling stations?

Analysis

4 Why did no one discuss politics?
5 These elections were a turning point in South African history, like the Sharpeville Massacre and the Soweto Uprising. Why?

Project

6 Find out about the political parties in South Africa on the internet. Which parties can you find? What are their aims and political philosophies?

13 Nelson Mandela

Nelson Mandela's statement at his presidential inauguration*

The ANC won the first free elections in 1994 gaining 62.65% of the votes and 252 seats in parliament. Their candidate was Nelson Mandela (see p. 27) who was inaugurated at the Union buildings in Pretoria on 10 May 1994. Many politicians from all over the world as well as members of royal families attended the ceremony. In his speech Nelson Mandela outlined the philosophy of a new democratic South Africa. – www.sahistory.org.za/pages/people/special%20projects/mandela/speeches/1990s/1994/1994_his_inauguration.htm.

Today, all of us do, by our presence here, and by our celebrations in other parts of our country and the world, confer glory and hope to newborn liberty.

Out of the experience of an extraordinary human disaster that lasted too long, must be born a society of which all humanity will be proud.

Our daily deeds as ordinary South Africans must produce an actual South African reality that will reinforce humanity's belief in justice, strengthen its confidence in the nobility of the human soul and sustain all our hopes for a glorious life for all.

All this we owe both to ourselves and to the peoples of the world who are so well represented here today.

To my compatriots, I have no hesitation in saying that each one of us is as intimately attached to the soil of this beautiful country as are the famous jacaranda trees of Pretoria and the mimosa trees of the bushveld.

Each time one of us touches the soil of this land, we feel a sense of personal renewal. The national mood changes as the seasons change.

We are moved by a sense of joy and exhilaration when the grass turns green and the flowers bloom.

That spiritual and physical oneness we all share with this common homeland explains the depth of the pain we all carried in our hearts as we saw our country tear itself apart in a terrible conflict, and as we saw it spurned, outlawed and isolated by the peoples of the world, precisely because it has become the universal base of the pernicious ideology and practice of racism and racial oppression. [...]

Mandela's inauguration: Thabo Mbeki is on his left, Frederik Willem de Klerk on his right

We deeply appreciate the role that the masses of our people and their political mass democratic, religious, women, youth, business, traditional and other leaders have played to bring about this conclusion. Not least among them is my Second Deputy President, the Honourable F.W. de Klerk.

We would also like to pay tribute to our security forces, in all their ranks, for the distinguished role they have played in securing our first democratic elections and the transition to democracy, from blood-thirsty forces which still refuse to see the light.

The time for the healing of the wounds has come.

The moment to bridge the chasms that divide us has come.

The time to build is upon us.

We have, at last, achieved our political emancipation. We pledge ourselves to liberate all our people from the continuing bondage of poverty, deprivation, suffering, gender and other discrimination.

We succeeded to take our last steps to freedom in conditions of relative peace. We commit ourselves to the construction of a complete, just and lasting peace.

We have triumphed in the effort to implant hope in the breasts of the millions of our people. We enter into a covenant that we shall build the society in which all South Africans, both black and white, will be able to walk tall, without any fear in their hearts, assured of their inalienable right to human dignity – a rainbow nation at peace with itself and the world.

As a token of its commitment to the renewal of our country, the new Interim Government of National Unity will, as a matter of urgency, address the issue of amnesty for various categories of our people who are currently serving terms of imprisonment.

We dedicate this day to all the heroes and heroines in this country and the rest of the world who sacrificed in many ways and surrendered their lives so that we could be free.

Their dreams have become reality. Freedom is their reward.

We are both humbled and elevated by the honour and privilege that you, the people of South Africa, have bestowed on us, as the first President of a united, democratic, non-racial and non-sexist government.

We understand it still that there is no easy road to freedom.

We know it well that none of us acting alone can achieve success.

We must therefore act together as a united people, for national reconciliation, for nation building, for the birth of a new world.

Let there be justice for all.
Let there be peace for all.
Let there be work, bread, water and salt for all.
Let each know that for each the body, the mind and the soul have been freed to fulfill themselves. Never, never and never again shall it be that this beautiful land will again experience the oppression of one by another and suffer the indignity of being the skunk of the world.
Let freedom reign.
The sun shall never set on so glorious a human achievement!

God bless Africa!

Vocabulary

3 to confer (v.): to officially give s.o a title etc, esp. as a reward for s.th. they have achieved - **10 to sustain** (v.): to make s.th. continue to exist over a period of time - **14 compatriot** (n.): s.o. who was born in or is a citizen of the same country as s.o. else - **22 to exhilarate** (v.): to make s.o. feel very excited and happy - **36 pernicious** (adj.): very harmful or evil, often in a way that you do not notice easily - **53 chasm** (n.): a very deep space between two high areas of rock, esp. one that is dangerous - **58 deprivation** (n.): a lack of s.th. that you need or want - **65 covenant** (n.): a formal agreement between two or more people - **70 token** (n.): s.th. that represents a feeling, fact, event etc - **81 to elevate** (v.): to give s.o. or s.th. a more important rank or position than they had before - **83 to bestow** (v.): to give s.o. s.th. of great value or importance - **90 reconciliation** (n.): a situation in which two people, countries etc become friendly with each other again after quarrelling

The Union Buildings in Pretoria

Explanations

45 Frederik Willem de Klerk (*1936): South African president from 1989-1994 and a member of the National Party. He released many political prisoners and unbanned resistance movements. He was also the main negotiator together with Mandela in achieving a democratic South Africa.

Awareness

1 Imagine that you have been elected the president of your country. Formulate a convincing speech that includes your aims for your term in office.

Comprehension

2 What does Mandela hope that his speech will achieve?
3 Who are his main addressees?

Analysis

4 Why does Mandela use "we" instead of "I"?
5 Why does he stress the beauty of the country?
6 What rhetorical means does Mandela use in his speech? What is their function?

Opinion

7 What do you find remarkable about this speech? Justify your opinion.

Project

8 Compare this speech with Barack Obama's speech at his inauguration in January 2009.
Can you find similarities?
What differences are there between the two speeches? Explain the differences.
What is the main function of both speeches? Do they have any aims in common?
What does Obama want to achieve for his country?

US president Barack Obama

14 Antjie Krog

Country of My Skull

Antjie Krog (*1952) is best known for her poetry in Afrikaans, although she has also written a short novel, a play and two other books, *Country of My Skull* (1998) and *A Change of Tongue* (2003). She translated Nelson Mandela's autobiography *Long Walk to Freedom* into Afrikaans. *Country of My Skull* is a reflection of her work as an SABC (South African Broadcasting Cooperation) radio journalist covering the TRC (Truth and Reconciliation Commission). The book uses both fictional and factual elements to deal with key issues such as history, culture, identity, nation building and how to deal with the apartheid past. These issues are multi-layered and reflect the complexities of nation building in the new South Africa. The following passage gives an insight into the key concepts she explores in her book. – Antjie Krog, *Country of My Skull* (London: Vintage, 1999), pp. 133f., 144, 361f., 422.

While a building is being destroyed in front of me by a beautiful, all-consuming fire – I argue with myself, I compare versions of truth.

Out of this must now be taken: The Truth?

It must be so.

The truth is validated by the majority, they say. Or you bring your own version of the truth to the merciless arena of the past – only in this way does the past become thinkable, the world become habitable.

And if you believe your own version, your own lie – because as narrators we all give ourselves permission to believe our own versions – how can it be said that you are being misleading? To what extent can you bring yourself not to know what you know? Eventually it is not the lie that matters, but that mechanism in yourself that allows you to accept distortions.

Either Hechter or Mamasela killed Irene Mutase. The truth does not lie in between. There cannot be a compromise between the two versions.

Is the truth known only to the dead?

Between the bodies, the child Tshidiso remains. Which truth does he inherit? It is for him that the truth must be found.

And so, if the truth is to be believed in this country, it must perhaps be written by those who bear the consequences of the past.

It is asking too much that everyone should believe the Truth Commission's version of the Truth. Or that people should be set free by this truth, should be healed and reconciled. But perhaps these narratives alone are enough to justify the existence of the Truth Commission. Because of these narratives, people can no longer indulge in their separate dynasties of denial. [...]

What do I do with this? They [the Vlakplaas Five] are as familiar as my brothers, cousins and school friends. Between us all distance is erased. Was there perhaps never a distance except the one I have built up with great effort within myself over the years? From the faces alone I can tell who was taken up in the Broederbond, who is a Rapportryer, a Ruiterwag, who is working class. The Mentzes, I know, have a musical bloodline. Whether your name is Jack or Paul or Johannes – it means something. In some way or another, all Afrikaners are related. If somebody says his father bought land here, or he grew up in Odendaalsrus or Welkom – then I know. From the accents I can guess where they buy their clothes, where they go on holiday, what car they drive, what music they listen to. What I have in common with them is a culture – and part of that culture over decades hatched the abominations for which they are responsible.

In a sense it is not these men but a culture that is asking for amnesty. [...]

I say: "Was Apartheid the product of some horrific shortcoming in Afrikaner culture? Could one find the key to this in Afrikaner songs and literature, in beer and braaivleis? How do I live with the fact that all the words used to humiliate, all the orders given to kill, belonged to the language of my heart? At the hearings, many of the victims faithfully reproduced these parts of their stories in Afrikaans as proof of the bloody fingerprints upon them." "Jung talks about inferiority. Do you know about that?"

"All I know is that my grandfather wanted to send my mother to Rhodes University so that she could learn to speak English 'better than an Englishman' – and that my mother refused. She told him she doesn't [sic] *need* to speak English better than an Englishman. But why do you ask about inferiority. Do you think Afrikaners are suffering from it?"

Antjie Krog

"According to Jung inferiority leads to a hysterical dissociation of the personality, which consists essentially in, as he puts it, wanting to jump over one's shadow, and looking for everything dark, inferior and culpable not in oneself but in others. That is why the hysteric always complains of being surrounded by inferior mischief-makers, a crowd of sub-men who should be exterminated so that the Superman can live at his high level of perfection. All men are dangerous if their leaders have unlimited power."

"It feels to me that if you look at the past only from the viewpoint of the victim, or the viewpoint of the perpetrator, the ultimate consequence is hatred ..."

"Are you grieving?"

His eyes are dark. An afternoon of limpid light turns into tatters of grey and twilight.

"How can I? What have I lost? Why do I feel I am gaining all the time? One does not grieve for Apartheid. Should I grieve for a phantom fatherland perhaps? I think ultimately I feel I don't have the right to grieve for the dead – I should rather take responsibility for the oppressors."

According to psychiatrist C. G. Jung a personal inferiority can be projected on others

In a wild arch of air I rock with the Commissioners in the boat back to the mainland. I am filled with an indescribable tenderness towards this Commission. With all its mistakes, its arrogance, its racism, its sanctimony, its incompetence, the lying, the failure to get an interim reparation policy off the ground after two years, the showing off – with all of this – it has been so brave, so naively brave in the winds of deceit, rancour and hate. Against a flood crashing with the weight of a brutalizing past on to new usurping politics, the Commission has kept alive the idea of a common humanity. Painstakingly it has chiselled a way beyond racism and made space for all of our voices. For all its failures, it carries a flame of hope that makes me proud to be from here, of here.

Info

TRC

The Truth and Reconciliation Commission (TRC) began its work in 1995. Its overall task was to deal with the atrocities that occurred during apartheid and between 1990 and 1994. It consisted of three committees: The Human Rights' Violations Committee investigated atrocities; the Amnesty Committee collected and processed applications for amnesty by over 7000 individuals; and finally the Reparations and Rehabilitation Committee advised the government on compensation for victims. The underlying principles were basically taken from Christian beliefs (the idea of healing and the ability to forgive) and the South African philosophy of ubuntu (there is no precise definition of ubuntu but it stands for humaneness, caring and community and derives from the Xhosa expression "Umuntu ngumuntu ngabanye Bantu" [People are people through other people]. The final report was presented to President Nelson Mandela in 1998, though the entire work of the TRC had not yet been completed; it continued until 2001.

Vocabulary

9 habitable (adj.): good enough for people to live in - **16 distortion** (n.): to explain a fact, statement, idea etc in a way that changes its real meaning - **22 to inherit** (v.): to have a problem caused by mistakes that other people have made in the past - **54 abomination** (n.): s.o. or s.th. that is extremely offensive or unacceptable - **61 to humiliate** (v.): /hjuˈmɪlieɪt/ to make s.o. feel ashamed and upset, esp. by making them seem stupid or weak - **76 dissociation** (n.): to do or say s.th. to show that you do not agree with a person or organisation - **80 culpable** (adj.): deserving blame - **98 to gain** (v.): to obtain or achieve s.th. important or valuable - **108 sanctimony** (n.): behaving as if you are morally better than other people, in a way that is annoying - **114 rancour** (n.): a feeling of hatred, esp. when you cannot forgive s.o. - **117 to usurp** (v.): to take s.o. else's power, position, job etc when you do not have the right to - **119 to chisel** (v.): /ˈtʃɪzəl/ to use a chisel; metal tool with a sharp edge, used to cut wood or stone

Explanations

Introduction: **Afrikaans**: see p. 10 - **17 Captain Jacques Hechter**: one of the so called Vlakplaas Five. He was responsible for and involved in numerous killings of people. Like Mamasela he was one of the killers of the Mutases. As his name indicates he belongs to the group of Afrikaners (see p. 5). - **17 Joe Mamasela**: an African (see p. 5) and a Vlakplaas askari (former member of one of the armed wings of oppositional movements such as the MK (see p. 26) who were "converted" by the Security Branch and became traitors against their own people). Mamasela is one of the notorious killers who worked at Vlakplaas and was involved in numerous killings. He was part of the killing of Robert und Irene Mutase. - **17 Irene Mutase**: wife of Robert Mutase. She was killed together with her husband at their home in the township of Temba, near Hammanskraal, by the Security Branch. The motive for killing the Mutases remains unknown. Robert Mutase was probably suspected of being too lenient with the opposition, or of being a traitor, and therefore was eliminated. - **21 Tshidiso**: the young son of Robert and Irene Mutase who survived the attack on their home. - **37 Vlakplaas Five**: Vlakplaas was a farm near Pretoria. It was used by members of the Security Branch to torture and kill opponents. Vlakplaas is a notorious place that stands for the cruelty of the methods used by the apartheid government to get rid off its enemies. Five specific Security Branch policemen are meant by the Vlakplaas Five: Captain Jacques Hechter, Paul van Vuuren, Captain Wouter Mentz, Roelf Venter and Jack Cronje. - **43 Afrikaaner Broederbond (AB)**: founded in 1918 to promote Afrikaner (see p. 5) culture and unity, it was a secret organisation supporting racial segregation. The AB was conservative and became very influential during apartheid: members of parliament and ministers were high ranking members of the organisation; the literal meaning is "league/confederation of brothers". - **44 Rapportryer / Ruiterwag**: both are conservative youth organisations belonging to the Afrikaner Broederbond; Ruiterwag literally means "horserider guard", Rapportryer can be translated as "dispatch rider". - **45 Mentzes**: an old Afrikaner (see p. 5) family - **47 Afrikaner**: see p. 5 - **49 Odendaalsrus**: a town in the Free State - **49 Welkom**: the second largest town in the Free State - **60 braaivleis**: barbecue; the literal meaning is "grilled meat" - **65 Carl Gustav Jung** (1875-1961): Swiss psychiatrist. He founded the school of analytical psychology. - **68 Rhodes University**: a prestigious university with a world-wide reputation for the high quality of education situated in Grahamstown, Eastern Cape. Grahamstown was founded in 1812 and was a frontier town where British immigrants settled in 1820.

Awareness

1 Compare South Africa's situation after the era of apartheid with that of Germany (after the Holocaust). What similarities and what differences can you find?

Comprehension

2 How does Krog define truth?
3 What does Krog say about the perpetrators of the apartheid system?
4 What does she have in common with them?

Analysis

5 How does Krog evaluate the TRC in *Country of My Skull* according to the text?
6 Analyse the sentence "In a sense it is not these men but a culture that is asking for amnesty." (ll. 55f.).
7 Comment on the importance of language (see also the chapter on the Soweto Uprising).
8 Which aspects of Afrikaner (see p. 5) culture are highlighted? Explain why they are highlighted.
9 What does Krug attempt to achieve for herself by writing this text?

Opinion

10 Do you think that establishing a commission like the TRC is a good and sufficient measure to deal with the past? Justify your opinion.
11 Discuss the following aspects of the TRC in class:
Can you imagine what kind of problems arose in connection with the TRC?
What does "truth" mean in the context of the TRC?
How do you think can reconciliation be achieved in South Africa?

Internet Projects

12 Find out more about the TRC and its proceedings on the following website: http://www.doj.gov.za/trc/. Work in groups of 4-5, find testimonies by victims and perpetrators and analyse them. How are they interviewed? What language policy was used by the TRC? Have a look at the number of amnesties that were granted. How many were not granted and for what reasons?
13 Zapiro (see p. 42) is one of the best-known cartoonists in South Africa and has an official website on the internet (www.zapiro.com). Find other cartoons concerned with South Africa, describe and analyse them.

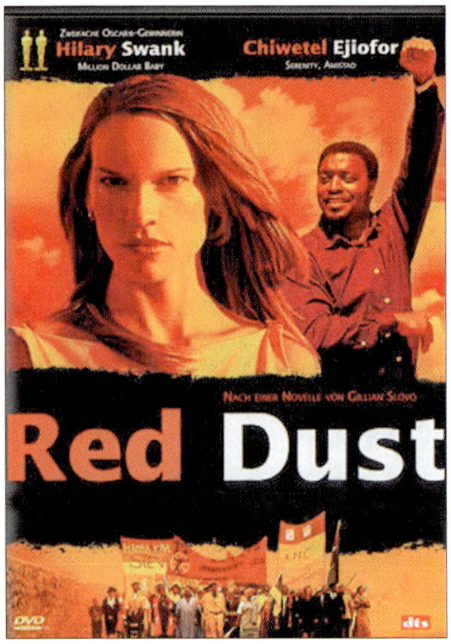

FILM ANALYSIS

14 The Film *Red Dust* (2004) is concerned with the TRC and its proceedings. It is based on the novel with the same title by Gillian Slovo and focuses on the relationship between victims and perpetrators. Watch the film in class. What do you learn about the TRC? Describe the relationship between Alex Mpondo and Dirk Hendricks. What is unusual about it? To what extent does the film criticise the proceedings of the TRC?

CARTOON

15 Describe the cartoon in detail. What aspects of the TRC are mentioned? Which problems are highlighted?

16 What do you think about the cartoon? Justify your opinion.

15 Thabo Mbeki

Statement on behalf of the ANC*

After the fall of apartheid, the issue of identity in the new South Africa became important on both national and individual levels. The "old" framework which categorised people along racial lines, and considered white notions of identity as the dominant and desirable ones, was discarded to make way for a broader concept of identity. Throughout his presidency Thabo Mbeki promoted the idea of an "African Renaissance". This included a return to African traditions, concepts of thought and societal values. His statement on behalf of the ANC (African National Congress) on the occasion of the adoption by the constitutional assembly of "The Republic of South Africa Constitution Bill 1996", in Cape Town, 8 May 1996 reflects the importance of identity and history in the political process of nation building. – www.anc.org.za/ancdocs/history/mbeki/1996/sp960508.html.

African identity

On an occasion such as this, we should, perhaps, start from the beginning.

So, let me begin.

I am an African.

I owe my being to the hills and the valleys, the mountains and the glades, the rivers, the deserts, the trees, the flowers, the seas and the ever-changing seasons that define the face of our native land.

My body has frozen in our frosts and in our latter day snows. It has thawed in the warmth of our sunshine and melted in the heat of the midday sun. The crack and the rumble of the summer thunders, lashed by startling lightning [sic], have been a cause both of trembling and of hope.

The fragrances of nature have been as pleasant to us as the sight of the wild blooms to the citizens of the veld.

The dramatic shapes of the Drakensberg, the soil-coloured waters of the Lekoa, iGqili noThukela, and the sands of the Kgalagadi, have all been panels of the set on the natural stage on which we act out the foolish deeds of the theatre of our day.

At times, and in fear, I have wondered whether I should concede equal citizenship of our country to the leopard and the lion, the elephant and the springbok, the hyena, the black mamba and the pestilential mosquito.

A human presence among all these, a feature on the face of our native land thus defined, I know that none dare challenge me when I say – I am an African!

I owe my being to the Khoi and the San whose desolate souls haunt the great expanses of the beautiful Cape – they who fell victim to the most merciless genocide our native land has ever seen, they who were the first to lose their lives in the struggle to defend our freedom and independence and they who, as a people, perished in the result.

Today, as a country, we keep an audible silence about these ancestors of the generations that live, fearful to admit the horror of a former deed, seeking to obliterate from our memories a cruel occurrence which, in its remembering, should teach us not and never to be inhuman again.

I am formed of the migrants who left Europe to find a new home on our native land. Whatever their own actions, they remain still part of me.

In my veins courses the blood of the Malay slaves who came from the East. Their proud dignity informs my bearing, their culture a part of my essence. The stripes they bore on their bodies from the lash of the slave master are a reminder embossed on my consciousness of what should not be done.

I am the grandchild of the warrior men and women that Hintsa and Sekhukhune led, the patriots that Cetshwayo and Mphephu took to battle, the soldiers Moshoeshoe and Ngungunyane taught never to dishonour the cause of freedom.

My mind and my knowledge of myself is formed by the victories that are the jewels in our African crown, the victories we earned from Isandhlwana to Khartoum, as Ethiopians and as the Ashanti of Ghana, as the Berbers of the desert.

I am the grandchild who lays fresh flowers on the Boer graves at St Helena and the Bahamas, who sees in the mind's eye and suffers the suffering of a simple peasant folk, death, concentration camps, destroyed homesteads, a dream in ruins.

I am the child of Nongqause. I am he who made it possible to trade in the world markets in diamonds, in

Thabo Mbeki, right, and Nelson Mandela celebrating their victory

gold, in the same food for which my stomach yearns.

I come of those who were transported from India and China, whose being resided in the fact, solely, that they were able to provide physical labour, who taught me that we could both be at home and be foreign, who taught me that human existence itself demanded that freedom was a necessary condition for that human existence.

Being part of all these people, and in the knowledge that none dare contest that assertion, I shall claim that – I am an African.

I have seen our country torn asunder as these, all of whom are my people, engaged one another in a titanic battle, the one redress a wrong that had been caused by one to another and the other, to defend the indefensible.

I have seen what happens when one person has superiority of force over another, when the stronger appropriate to themselves the prerogative even to annul the injunction that God created all men and women in His image.

I know what if signifies when race and colour are used to determine who is human and who, sub-human.

I have seen the destruction of all sense of self-esteem, the consequent striving to be what one is not, simply to acquire some of the benefits which those who had improved themselves as masters had ensured that they enjoy.

I have experience of the situation in which race and colour is used to enrich some and impoverish the rest. [...]

I am an African!

Because of that, I am also able to state this fundamental truth that I am born of a people who are heroes and heroines.

I am born of a people who would not tolerate oppression.

The dramatic shapes of the Drakensberg

I am of a nation that would not allow that fear of death, torture, imprisonment, exile or persecution should result in the perpetuation of injustice.

The great masses who are our mother and father will not permit that the behaviour of the few results in the description of our country and people as barbaric.

Patient because history is on their side, these masses do not despair because today the weather is bad. Nor do they turn triumphalist when, tomorrow, the sun shines.

Whatever the circumstances they have lived through and because of that experience, they are determined to define for themselves who they are and who they should be.

We are assembled here today to mark their victory in acquiring and exercising their right to formulate their own definition of what it means to be African.

The importance of the constitution

The constitution whose adoption we celebrate constitutes an unequivocal statement that we refuse to accept that our Africanness shall be defined by our race, colour, gender of historical origins.

It is a firm assertion made by ourselves that South Africa belongs to all who live in it, black and white.

It gives concrete expression to the sentiment we share as Africans, and will defend to the death, that the people shall govern.

It recognises the fact that the dignity of the individual is both an objective which society must pursue, and is a goal which cannot be separated from the material well-being of that individual.

It seeks to create the situation in which all our people shall be free from fear, including the fear of the oppression of one national group by another, the fear of the disempowerment of one social echelon by another, the fear of the use of state power to deny anybody their fundamental human rights and the fear of tyranny.

It aims to open the doors so that those who were disadvantaged can assume their place in society as equals with their fellow human beings without regard to colour, race, gender, age or geographic dispersal.

It provides the opportunity to enable each one and all to state their views, promote them, strive for their implementation in the process of governance without fear that a contrary view will be met with repression.

It creates a law-governed society which shall be inimical to arbitrary rule.

It enables the resolution of conflicts by peaceful means rather than resort to force.

It rejoices in the diversity of our people and creates the space for all of us voluntarily to define ourselves as one people.

As an African, this is an achievement of which I am proud, proud without reservation and proud without any feeling of conceit.

Our sense of elevation at this moment also derives from the fact that this magnificent product is the unique creation of African hands and African minds.

But it is also constitutes a tribute to our loss of vanity that we could, despite the temptation to treat ourselves as an exceptional fragment of humanity, draw on the accumulated experience and wisdom of all humankind, to define for ourselves what we want to be.

Vocabulary

21 panel (n.): a flat piece of wood, glass etc with straight sides which forms part of a door, wall, fence etc - **31 desolate** (adj.): s.o. who is desolate feels very sad and lonely - **33 genocide** (n.): the deliberate murder of a whole group or race of people - **40 to obliterate** (v.): to remove a thought, feeling, or memory from s.o.'s mind - **51 to emboss** (v.): to make a raised pattern on the surface of metal, paper, leather etc - **66 peasant** (adj.): s.o. in a poor country or in former times, who does farm work on the piece of land where they live - **70 to yearn** (v.): literary to have a strong desire for s.th., esp. s.th. that is difficult or impossible to get - **72 solely** (adv.): not involving anything or anyone else; only - **78 assertion** (n.): s.th. that you say or write that you strongly believe - **80 asunder** (adv.): literary to be broken violently into many pieces - **86 prerogative** (n.): a right that s.o. has because of their importance or position - **86 to annul** (v.): technical to state that a marriage or legal agreement no longer exists - **107 to perpetuate** (v.): to make s.th. continue to exist for a long time - **138 echelon** (n.): a rank or level of responsibility in an organization, business etc, or the people at that level - **144 dispersal** (n.): the act of spreading things over a wide area - **148 repression** (n.): cruel and severe control of a large group of people - **150 inimical** (adj.): *fml.* very unfavourable for s.th.

Explanations

Introduction: **Thabo Mbeki**: He was born in 1942 in the Transkei and is the son of Govan Mbeki who was a leader of the ANC in the eastern Cape. Thabo joined the ANC

Youth League in 1956 and left the country after being detained in 1962. He returned to South Africa in the 1990s and rose in the ANC ranks. He became president of South Africa in June 1999. His presidency was overshadowed by his controversial remarks on HIV/AIDS and his attitude towards Zimbabwe's leader Robert Mugabe. He resigned as president in September 2008. - **Introduction**: **ANC**: see p. 17 - **31 Khoi, San**: see p. 8 - **54/55 Hintsa, Sekhukhuni, Moshoeshoe/Moshweshwe**: see p. 28 - **54 Cetshwayo**: c. 1826-1884, son of the Zulu king Mpande and chief of the Zulu. He fought against the British in the Anglo-Zulu War. He won the battle of Islandlawana in 1879, but was defeated afterwards. He flew to the Zulu capital Ulundi where he was captured by the British and was exiled to Cape Town. After visiting Queen Victoria in England, he was allowed to return to Zululand where he died shortly afterwards. - **55 Mphephu**: c. 1868-1924, chief of the Venda. He defended independence against Boer rule, but was defeated and had to flee to present-day Zimbabwe in 1898. - **56 Ngungunyane**: c. 1850-1906, Tsonga chief who was defeated by the Portuguese in 1895 - **68 Nongqause/ Nongqawuse**: 1841-1898, Xhosa prophetess. She predicted that the Xhosa would regain their land from the whites by killing their cattle and burning their fields to appease the ancestors. This became known in history as the Xhosa Cattle Killing (1856). The slaughtering of the cattle and the loss of crops had a devastating effect on the Xhosa nation and did not bring the wished - for expulsion of the colonialists.

Info

The election in 2009

The latest election in South Africa took place on 22 April 2009. 77% of the population went to the polling stations. The ANC gained 65.9 % of the votes while the main opposition party, Democratic Alliance (DA), won 16.66 %. The ANC did not gain a two thirds majority in parliament which would have been a prerequisite to enable them to change the constitution.

The election attracted international attention because it was supposed that the results of the election might cause a shift in South African government policy. The reason for this is the ANC leader Jacob Zuma, who is the next president of the country and will remain in office for five years. Zuma has provoked much controversy in South Africa. In 2005 he was accused of rape and corruption. In both cases the charges were withdrawn. In addition, a clash of ideologies within the ANC between Zuma and Mbeki supporters led to Mbeki's resignation in September 2008 and to the splitting of the party. The breakaway party is called Cope (Congress of the People) and is under the leadership of Mosiuoa "Terror" Lekota. Cope opposes Zuma's popularist approach.

Awareness

1 What is your nationality? How important is it for your identity?

Comprehension

2 Which turning points in South Africa's history are mentioned in this speech?
3 How does Mbeki evaluate the constitution?

Analysis

4 Analyse the structure of the speech.
5 What does Mbeki say about his own identity? Why does he mention his own identity?
6 Why does he identify himself as an African, not a South African?

Opinion

7 How does Mbeki try to arouse emotions? Why does he appeal to his listeners' emotions?
8 Why does he explain his African identity in a speech that refers to the new constitution?

Projects

9 Find out more about the South African constitution of 1996. Look at the second text, the Bill of Rights. What rights are granted here? Compare your findings with the demands in the Freedom Charter (pp. 19f.). Does the Bill of Rights of the constitution fulfil the demands of the Freedom Charter? If so, to what extent? (see http://www.info.gov.za/documents/constitution/1996/96cons2.htm)
10 The South African constitution is often quoted as being the most modern and democratic in the world. From your reading of the Bill of Rights, do you agree with this statement? Justify your opinion.
11 Compare Mbeki's speech with Mandela's speech at the Rivonia Trial (see pp. 26f.). To what extent do they differ? Can you find any similarities? Why do both stress the African heritage?

16

Zakes Mda

"Outsiders"

In the following text Zakes Mda explores the fear many South Africans have of "foreigners" from other parts of Africa with whom they live side by side in the townships or in the inner city areas like Hillbrow in Johannesburg. – Heidi Holland/Adam Roberts (ed.), *From Jo'burg to Jozi. Stories about Africa's infamous city* (London: Penguin, 2002), pp. 166-168.

Skyline of Johannesburg, South Africa's biggest city

It would be wrong to say nothing has changed since liberation in 1994. Although the squatter camps have become much bigger because the new rulers abolished influx control laws that prohibited black people from coming to Johannesburg unless they were employed, the government is working hard to house the homeless. New low-income houses are coming up where it used to be nothing but veld. Or where it used to be makeshift corrugated iron and cardboard shelters in the middle of a quagmire. The government gives the homeless people, who are either unemployed or who receive too small an income to afford accommodation, a subsidy to build their own houses. Some people have criticised this state welfarism because it creates a dependency mentality among the poor. They tend to look to the government to provide them with everything. The government carries on with its housing programme, and thousands of previously homeless people now have houses of their own. Still the government, with its meagre resources, is not able to house everybody. The homeless are still the bane of the inner city.

Unemployment and homelessness have tended to cause a lot of xenophobia among the poor Johannesburgers. The scapegoat is always the foreigner. Everyone who looks vaguely like a foreigner is regarded as an illegal immigrant. Especially if they are darker in complexion than the "average South African" – whatever that means. South Africa's xenophobia is really racism. South Africans – both black and white – don't hate and fear all foreigners. Only black foreigners from the rest of Africa and from the United States of America. White foreigners from Europe and the Americas are welcomed with open arms. The impression that is created is that black foreigners come to steal local jobs whereas white foreigners are bringing Investment into the country.

This, of course, is a fallacy born of South Africa's old apartheid past. Black South Africans long internalised self-hate. Hence their mistrust and suspicion of fellow black Africans. The government and non-governmental organisations that are run by the more enlightened South Africans are trying very hard to fight this attitude. Of course most members of the government were in exile in other countries in Africa where they received assistance to fight their war of liberation. They therefore are embarrassed by their compatriots' xenophobia. Many campaigns continue to be waged through the mass media to wean the people of Johannesburg and South Africa from this xenophobia.

One big fallacy is that black foreigners come to Johannesburg to steal jobs from the locals. Many people from the north of South Africa come to this country as political refugees. Many of them are professional people who nevertheless don't get jobs in their professions. Instead they create jobs for themselves. It is not unusual to drive into a shopping mall in one of the suburbs of Johannesburg and find that the parking attendants are lawyers or teachers from Congo. Or from any of the French-speaking countries of central and west Africa.

One of these lawyers was my shoemaker at a street corner in Melville. Although he learned shoe repairing as an emergency when he arrived in Johannesburg and couldn't get a job in his profession, he managed to do it well. Many people brought their shoes to him. Soon he employed other people. Now he runs a big store of his own, selling all sorts of locally made and imported shoes. That is how many of the foreigners from the African countries start. They are very enterprising. They are not afraid to start doing menial jobs that locals are loath to touch. Then they grow and end up creating employment for the very South Africans who despise them.

Gold in the streets of Johannesburg may be an illusion for many South Africans who flock into this city from other towns and villages, but many foreigners from the rest of Africa have found it through their hard work and enterprising spirit. They have found it in the businesses that they have established from zero. Businesses that end up employing many South Africans.

Zakes Mda is also known by the names "Zanemvula Kizito Gatyeni Mda", "Zanemvula Mda" and "Zanemvula Kizito Gatyeni". He was born in Herschel (Eastern Cape) in October 1948 and received his academic education at Ohio University (USA) and the University of Cape Town where he obtained his doctorate in 1989. During apartheid he was arrested in the 1960s for his anti-apartheid activities and went into exile in the 1970s. Today he is a lecturer, playwright and writer and divides his time between the USA and South Africa. His novels and plays focus on issues faced by modern Africans in South Africa. His most recent novels are *Heart of Redness* (2001), *Madonna of Excelsior* (2002), *The Whale Caller* (2005), and *Cion* (2007).

Vocabulary

2 squatter (n.): s.o. who lives in an empty building or on a piece of land without permission and without paying rent - **4 to prohibit** (v.): to officially stop an activity by making it illegal or against the rules - **8 veld** (n.): the high flat area of land in South Africa that is covered in grass and has few trees - **8 makeshift** (adj.): made for temporary use when you need s.th. and there is nothing better available - **10 quagmire** (n.): an area of soft wet muddy ground - **12 subsidy** (n.): money that is paid by a government or organization to make prices lower, reduce the cost of producing goods etc - **14 welfarism** (n.): a way of life in which s.o. does not work, but accepts money from the government and makes no attempt to improve their situation - **21 bane** (n.): s.th. that causes trouble or makes people unhappy - **40 fallacy** (n.): a false idea or belief, esp. one that a lot of people believe is true - **73 enterprising** (adj.): showing the ability to think of new activities or ideas and make them work - **74 menial** (adj.): menial work is boring, needs no skill, and is not important - **74 loath** (adj.): unwilling to do s.th.

Explanations

Introduction: **Hillbrow**: inner city suburb of Johannesburg. In the past it was known for its cultural importance and diversity; a lot of artists and ethnicities lived there. After apartheid too many people moved into the high rise flats of Hillbrow while the original owners moved out. Today Hillbrow is a rundown area where refugees, people from the townships and rural areas live together. It is marked by poverty and decay. - **23 xenophobia**: The word derives from the Greek words: "xenos" which means foreigner and "phobia" that stands for fear. Xenophobia is thus the fear of foreigners. South Africa has always been a place to seek work. There was a steady influx of people from the southern African countries, mainly to the mines around Johannesburg. Since South Africa's transformation into a democracy the country has become a "Mecca" for many other African people searching for work, a stable economy, security, refuge, and peace. The South African people, who were formerly oppressed by the apartheid system and its lasting consequences such as lack of education or job opportunities, feel threatened by these "newcomers".

Awareness

1 What is the situation like in your country as far as xenophobia is concerned? What are the reasons for xenophobia in your country?

Comprehension

2 Which reasons are given for xenophobia in "Outsiders"?
3 Which changes were made by the new government?

Analysis

4 Summarise Mda's arguments.
5 What is peculiar about the kind of xenophobia described by Mda?
6 Why does Mda say that South African xenophobia is racist (l. 28)?
7 What kind of language does the author use in the text?
8 How does Mda evaluate foreigners in his country?

Opinion

9 To what extent do you agree or disagree with Mda's ideas and arguments? Justify your opinion.

Project

10 Find out more about the violent incidents that occurred around Johannesburg und Pretoria in May 2008. Read the following two newspaper articles about this violent outbreak of xenophobia. The first one is from a South African weekly (http://www.mg.co.za/article/2008-05-19-mob-violence-sweeps-gauteng), while the second was published in Britain (http://www.guardian.co.uk/world/2008/may/25/southafrica). Compare the two newspaper articles.
What is stressed in the British newspaper?
How do the victims of the attack perceive South Africa?
What is said about the situation of immigrants after the attacks?
Take both articles into consideration. Do you think the government did enough? Justify your opinion.

Cartoon Analysis

11 The cartoon captures the ironies involved in South African xenophobia. Describe the cartoon and comment on it. Can you think of a similar perception of refugees in your country?

Vocabulary

biopsy (n.): the removal of cells, liquid etc from the body of s.o. who is ill, in order to find out more about their disease and its effects - **negligence** (n.): failure to take enough care over s.th. that you are responsible for - **domicile** (n.): a place where s.o. lives - **interalia** (n.): (*Latin*) among other things

Explanation

dysplastic (adj.): dysplasia is a medical term and means abnormal growth or development

17

Phaswane Mpe

Welcome to Our Hillbrow

In Phaswane Mpe's *Welcome to Our Hillbrow* (2001) the reader follows the protagonist Refentse who comes from the rural areas and is confronted with the exciting and dangerous life in the inner city as embodied in the notorious district of Hillbrow (see p. 47) in postapartheid Johannesburg. In the following passage HIV/AIDS and where it might come from are discussed in a rather unusual way.
– *Welcome to Our Hillbrow* (Pietermaritzburg: University of Natal Press, 2001), pp. 3f.

The Hillbrow Tower (J. G. Strijdom Tower) is one of the landmarks of Johannesburg

One of the stories that you remember vividly was of a young man who died of a strange illness in 1990, when you were matriculating. The migrants said it could only have been AIDS. After all, was he not often seen roaming the whorehouses and dingy pubs of Hillbrow? While his poor parents imagined that he was working away in the city, in order to make sure that there would be a huge bag of maize meal to send back for all at the homestead. The migrants, most of whom insisted that he was a stubborn brother, who suffered because of blocking his ears with gum while they dished out advice to him, also said that he was often seen with Makwerekwere women, hanging onto his arms and dazzling him with sugar-coated kisses that were sure to destroy any man, let alone an impressionable youngster like him.

He died, poor chap; of what precisely, no one knew. But strange illnesses courted in Hillbrow, as Tiragalong knew only too well, could only translate into AIDS. This AIDS, according to popular understanding, was caused by foreign germs that travelled down from the central and western parts of Africa. More specifically, certain newspaper articles attributed the source of the virus that caused AIDS to a species called the Green Monkey, which people in some parts of West Africa were said to eat as meat, thereby contracting the disease. Migrants (who were Tiragalong's authoritative grapevine on all important issues) deduced from such media reports that AIDS's travel route into Johannesburg was through Makwerekwere; and Hillbrow was the sanctuary in which Makwerekwere basked.

There were others who went even further, saying that AIDS was caused by the bizarre sexual behaviour of the Hillbrowans.

How could any man have sex with another man? they demanded to know.

Those who claimed to be informed – although none could admit to having seen or practised it personally – said such sex was done anally. They also explained how it was done – dog style – to the disgust of most of the people of Tiragalong, who insisted that filth and sex should be two separate things.

Phaswane Mpe was born in the Limpopo Province in September 1970. He went to High School near Polokwane and studied at the University of the Witwatersrand, obtaining an M.A. in African Literature in 1996. He became a lecturer at the University of the Witwatersrand in Johannesburg. His debut novel *Welcome to Our Hillbrow* (2001) deals with postapartheid Johannesburg, xenophobia, HIV/AIDS and inner city life. He died unexpectedly in 2004. His short stories and poems were posthumously published in a book called *Brooding Clouds* (2008).

Vocabulary

26 to court (v.): *old-fashioned* if a man and a woman are courting they are having a romantic relationship - **29 germ** (n.): a bacterium that can make you ill - **34 to contract** (v.): to begin to have an illness - **35 grapevine** (n.): to hear about s.th. because the information has been passed from one person to another in conversation - **38 sanctuary** (n.): a peaceful place that is safe and provides protection - **39 to bask** (v.): to enjoy sitting or lying in the heat of the sun or the fire

Explanations

Title: **Hillbrow**: see p. 47 - **21 Makwerekwere**: derogatory term for foreigners - **26 Tiragalong**: fictitious village in the Northern Province of South Africa

The lady sitting next to Thabo Mbeki is the former health minister Manto Tshabalala-Msimang who was also notorious for her comments on HIV/AIDS (11 March 28, 2000)

Vocabulary/Explanation

AZT: abbreviation for "azidothymidine". It is a drug that delays the development of AIDS - **whacko**: *(colloquial)* crazy

Awareness

1 What do you know about HIV/AIDS? Collect your information using a mind map.

Comprehension

2 How is Hillbrow characterised by the people of Tiragalong and the narrator?
3 Who is the narrator addressing?

Analysis

4 What reasons are given for the cause of HIV/AIDS in the story?
5 Who are the "authorities" discussing HIV/AIDS?
6 What is remarkable about the language use in the passage? What is it trying to achieve?

Opinion

7 Why is a village (Tiragalong) contrasted with the urban area (Hillbrow, Johannesburg) in the passage?

Project

8 Read the complete novel. It gives you a good insight into the problems of South Africa, but also demonstrates the importance of Johannesburg as a city which reflects postapartheid and its characteristics. The novel also makes use of "magic realism". Find out how this literary device is defined. To what extent does the novel use this device? Why is it appropriate to use magic realism in the context of South Africa and its traditions?

Cartoon Analysis

9 Though the government under Mbeki denied the actual causes of HIV/AIDS, other South Africans disputed the official policy. Nelson Mandela is a good example: he used his popularity to raise money for the prevention of the epidemic and to support its victims who are often poor and destitute. The cartoon by Zapiro comments on this controversial issue. Analyse the cartoon in class. What is criticised regarding Mbeki's attitude towards the disease?

Info

Statistics - HIV and AIDS Estimates

The numbers and percentages given are based on research that was carried out by the UN. It shows the figures of HIV infections and deaths caused by AIDS in 2007. The numbers in brackets indicate the lowest and the highest estimates.

Number of people living with HIV: 5 700 000 [4 900 000 - 6 600 000]
Adults aged 15 to 49 prevalence rate: 18.1% [15.4% - 20.9%]
Adults aged 15 and up living with HIV: 5 400 000 [4 700 000 - 6 200 000]
Women aged 15 and up living with HIV: 3 200 000 [2 800 000 - 3 700 000]
Children aged 0 to 14 living with HIV: 280 000 [230 000 - 320 000]
Deaths due to AIDS: 350 000 [270 000 - 420 000]
Orphans due to AIDS aged 0 to 17: 1 400 000 [1 100 000 - 1 800 000]

Source: Epidemiological Fact Sheet on HIV and AIDS, 2008 found at:
http://www.unaids.org/en/CountryResponses/Countries/south_africa.asp

18 Crime-ridden South Africa*

Crime is a major issue in the new South Africa. An increase in crime is not unusual for a country in transition. In South Africa most serious crimes occur in the townships (see p. 28), but in certain areas it has also moved into city centres such as those of Johannesburg or Durban. Most incidences of serious crime, e.g. rape, aggravated robbery and murder, were committed shortly before and after the first free elections. Although the numbers are still high, the situation is gradually returning to normal. This newspaper article, which was taken from the weekly South African *Mail & Guardian*, highlights the difficulties of crime prevention in South Africa. - www.mg.co.za/article/2007-07-06-the-murder-capital-of-sa.

"Give me 10 more vehicles and 85 extra cops on the beat and I will take Nyanga off the number one murder spot in the country."

Assistant commissioner Manyano Noqayi of Nyanga police station was speaking this week after the area was, for the second consecutive year, named the neighbourhood with the highest number of murders in the country.

Crime statistics show the murder rate in the Western Cape is 2,5% higher than last year, with 303 murders reported in Nyanga in the past 11 months.

Three months ago Noqayi was tasked with policing the murder capital of South Africa. "As a priority we need to close down the known 558 illegal liquor outlets in Nyanga and only then can we start talking about turning around the crime problem," said Noqayi. He estimated that 90% of all murders, rapes and assaults in Nyanga were alcohol related.

Noqayi said tik (methamphetamine) was playing an increasing role in violent crimes in the area. "We estimate that about 95% of all murders and rapes happen between people known to each other and, while alcohol is the main substance of abuse, tik is increasingly involved – especially where rapes also occur," he said.

Resident Nomsa Kelem was born in Nyanga and, 29 years later, she still hates living there. "We're murdered by drunk kids in Nyanga. My neighbour was shot, killed and robbed for R12 cash and a pair of shoes by a gang of 15-year-old boys and the police couldn't get here because their cars can't drive between our shacks," said Kelem, who lives in Brown's Farm.

Kelem and her family are desperate to leave, but they have no idea where else to put up their shack. "We stay here because we're unemployed and if you live in a shack it doesn't matter where you live – it's all the same. The criminals find you and kill you and the plastic walls of your house can't protect you and neither can the cops," she said.

Kelem is one of 400 000 people officially known to be living in Nyanga. However, Noqayi reckoned the population was closer to a million. "There's about 10 people living in each shack – we work on the figure of policing close to a million people," he said. If Noqayi is correct, the police to resident ratio is one police officer for every 4 000 residents.

Noqayi acknowledged that large parts of Nyanga were not accessible by vehicle: "One of the most outstanding aspects of Nyanga is the lack of formal houses. By far the majority of dwellings are shacks and we have a disproportionate number of illegal shebeens; most of the murders happen at these places where liquor is sold, either when people are on their way to shebeens or when they leave these places."

Another problem, said Noqayi, was that the community still saw the police as the enemy. "The community is not involved yet in fighting crime. People are too scared to assist us and they've not bought into the concept of working with the cops."

Noqayi said a large percentage of the murder victims were killed by gangs of youths between 14 and 17 years old. There were no sports facilities and hardly any shops. Some streets were strewn with rubbish, rocks and pieces of concrete, that the community had piled up to keep vehicles out, deliberately turning them into no-go zones to try to keep out criminal elements.

Vocabulary

30 shack (n.): a small building that has not been built very well - **40 to reckon** (v.): to guess a number or amount, without calculating it exactly - **44 ratio** (n.): a relationship between two amounts that is represented by a pair of numbers showing how much greater one amount is than the other

Explanations

2 Nyanga: township near Cape Town. Nyanga means "moon". The township was built in 1948. - **9 f. Western Cape**: one of the provinces of South Africa. Cape Town belongs to this province. - **19 tik**: methamphetamine, a cheap drug that is easy to produce. It is inhaled by addicts and causes severe health damage. - **28 R12**: 12 Rand (South African currency) are about 1,20 € - **31 Brown's Farm**: informal settlement near Cape Town - **50 shebeen**: see p. 35

Awareness

1 What is the "murder capital" of your country? What do you know about it?

Comprehension

2 Who are the main groups of criminals in South Africa?

Analysis

3 Why do people like Nomsa Kelem stay in the crime-ridden townships?
4 Which reasons are given for crime in the townships?

Opinion

5 Can you imagine what could be done to fight crime in the townships? Justify your choice of measures.
6 The assistant commissioner in the article states that the community still sees the police as the enemy (ll. 54f.). Why do people hesitate to cooperate with the police? Justify your opinion.

Projects

7 Read the novel *Tsotsi* by Athol Fugard. The protagonist is a young and hardened criminal in Sophiatown. The novel is set in the apartheid years and reflects on the harshness of life in the townships. Why is the protagonist called "Tsotsi"? How is he characterised in the novel? Why does the baby change his life?
8 Compare the novel with the film by Gavin Hood (2005). The changes made for the film are significant. What differences between novel and film can you find? Can you think of reasons for these changes? Why does the setting of the film differ from that of the novel?

Film Analysis

9 The film *Tsotsi* is based on a novel by South African playwright Athol Fugard and focuses on the protagonist named Tsotsi who is the leader of a gang of young criminals in a township near Johannesburg. The term "tsotsi" means gangster. The film received the academy award (Oscar®) for best foreign language film in 2006. How is the issue "crime" dealt with in the film?
What reasons are given in the film for Tsotsi's criminal career?
Why does the baby change Tsotsi's behaviour?
Why does the audience develop sympathy with the protagonist?
How does the music influence the atmosphere in the film?

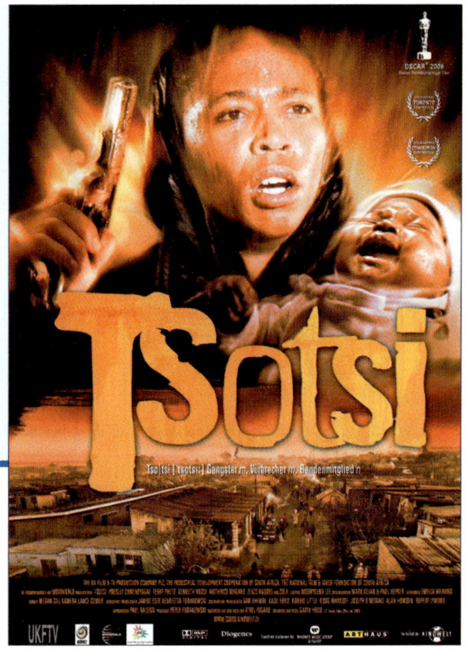

Tsotsi *is a film about criminal youngsters in the townships*

19

Hermann Giliomee / Bernard Mbenga

South Africa's economy in the 20th and 21st centuries*

The economy of a country is an important factor in its development and well-being, especially when a great change in the political system occurs. One of the most important tasks for the new South African government was to consolidate the opposition forces in the country and to lessen the gap between rich and poor. This also meant repealing unjust laws that promoted skilled jobs for whites, and removing exclusive white privileges. In addition the new government had to find ways of redistributing the wealth of the country. – Hermann Giliomee/ Bernard Mbenga: *New History of South Africa* (Cape Town: Tafelberg, 2007), pp. 433-435.

The economy in the 20th century

The prospects for social stability were closely tied to those of an expanding economy creating new jobs and some welfare benefits for the very poor. Since the early 1930s South Africa had burst the bonds of a struggling, neo-colonial economy in a race against time to provide food and work for its rapidly growing population. The gold mines were becoming less and less profitable, the manufacturing sector sluggish and agriculture was nearly swamped by its problems. Liberal historian C.W. de Kiewiet wrote that the backward economy of the early 1930s suffered from three factors that constrained growth: "its low-grade ore, low-grade land and low-grade [poorly educated] people". The South African economy at this point was not much different from the struggling economies that would characterise independent African states in the 1970s.

The 40 years of high growth between 1933 and 1973 were followed by stagnation after the Soweto uprising of 1976 and declining per capita incomes. After the first democratic election the economy picked up. Private fixed capital formation rose from 10% of Gross Domestic Product in 1993, to 26%, a level last seen in 1983 before serious unrest had begun.

The economy in the 21st century

By 2003 the South African economy had grown almost beyond recognition. It was now 33rd in the world for the largest industrial output, 27th for services output, the 21st biggest economy measured in purchasing power and the 18th largest in market capitalisation. But it was also in the top four for the highest rate of unemployment in developing economies, in the top three of the Gini coefficient league of inequality, in the top three for the murder rate and, because of the incidence of HIV-Aids, the one with the 21st highest death rate.

Economic problems

But in some respects the fundamental weaknesses of the economy and the political system remained. First, like other economies whose growth was driven by commodities (in the South African case it was minerals and agricultural products), South Africa failed to develop an exports-driven manufacturing sector. By 2006 it was recognised that South Africa could find itself in serious economic trouble if the worldwide boom in commodities suddenly faltered.

Second, the ruling party overspent in a dramatic effort to change materially the welfare of all segments of its constituency. Before the mid-1970s there was grossly disproportionate social welfare spending on whites. Having promised "a better life for all" in 1994, the ANC government tried to address the plight of the poor. It built on a fairly well-developed welfare system. In the final years of apartheid South Africa was already spending more, as a percentage of GDP, on social assistance in the form of non-contributory schemes than developed countries and more than almost any country in the developing southern hemisphere.

Between 2001 and 2005 the ANC government increased social security by an average annual rate of almost 26%. The recipients of all types of social grants jumped from just under three million in 2000 to just under eight million by the time of the 2004 election. By 2004 as many as 56% of households in the lowest living-standard category received grants and pensions. With twelve million people, or around a quarter of the population, receiving a direct cash transfer from the state, South Africa easily had the largest welfare system in the developing world. Mexico and Brazil paled in comparison. South Africa had become virtually the only welfare state in the developing world.

But without high economic growth, such a welfare net – and even more so, any extension of it – was unsustainable.

Ideology vs. economy

Also hampering the economy was the tendency of government, like its predecessor, to put ideological goals before efficiency, merit and growth. Before 1970 the obsession was with segregating society, after 1994 it was with black empowerment and the attempt to bring about demographic representation. Neither promised to accelerate job creation or reduce crime, the major preoccupations of the citizenry. Similarly the government's efforts to address the developmental problems of Africa deterred foreign fixed investment, which showed a downward trend. The state steadily expanded services in water, electricity and sanitation, but with half the economically active population out of work, many were unable to pay for the services and had them terminated.

Vocabulary

9 sluggish (adj.): moving or reacting more slowly than normal - **10 swamp** (v.): to suddenly give s.o. a lot of work, problems etc to deal with - **40 commodity** (n.): a product that can be sold to make a profit - **45 to falter** (v.): to become weaker and unable to continue in an effective way - **48 constituency** (n.): an area of the country that elects a representative to a parliament - **73 sustainable** (adj.): an action or process that is sustainable can continue or last for a long time - **75 to hamper** (v.): to restrict s.o.'s movements, activities, or achievements by causing difficulties for them - **77 merit** (n.): *fml.* a good quality that makes s.th. deserve praise or admiration - **80 demography** (n.): the study of human populations and the ways in which they change - **84 to deter** (v.): to persuade s.o. not to do s.th., by making them realize it will be difficult or will have unpleasant results

Explanations

32 Gini coefficient: a statistical measure developed by the Italian Corrado Gini. It is often used to represent inequality in wealth or income distribution of a country.

Awareness

1 Where does your country presently rank in the world economy?

Comprehension

2 Describe the development of the South African economy since the 1930s.
3 What economic problems were caused by apartheid?

Analysis

4 What are the major problems which South Africa's economy has to face right now?
5 What reasons are given for these problems?

Opinion

6 How would you cope with the gap between rich and poor in South Africa? What measures can you think of to improve the situation of the poor?

Project

7 Find out about South Africa's main resources or economic sectors. Which are the most promising ones? Explain why.
8 The chart shows the unemployment rates in South Africa from September 2001 to September 2007. The figures also reflect the unemployment of people according to their population group. Analyse the chart. What information can you gain from it about unemployment in South Africa?

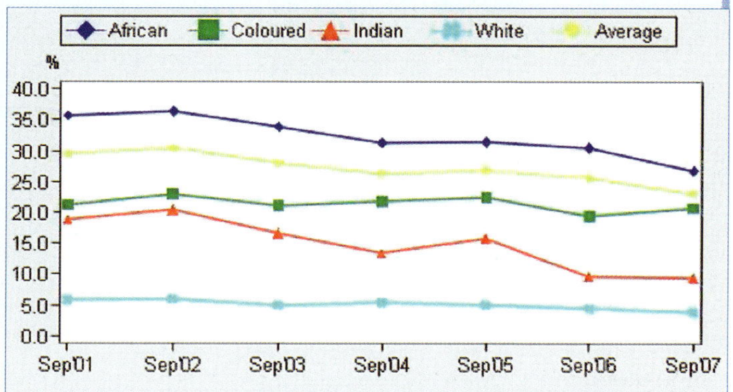

Source: www.statssa.gov.za/PublicationsHTML/P0210September2007/html/P0210September2007.html

20 Arthur Maimane

"The changing faces of Jo'burg"

Arthur Maimane (1932 – 2005) was an author and journalist and one of the famous and legendary *Drum* writers. He created a well-known detective figure called "The Chief" who survived in the townships on his wits and cleverness. The stories were published under the pseudonym "Arthur Mogale". Maimane also wrote a novel, *Victims* (1976), that was banned in South Africa and re-issued as *Hate No More* in 2000. In "The changing faces of Jo'burg" Arthur Maimane draws an interesting picture of Johannesburg in the past and the present. – Heidi Holland/Adam Roberts (ed.), *From Jo'burg to Jozi. Stories about Africa's infamous city* (London: Penguin, 2002), pp. 148-150.

Apartheid forced me into self-imposed exile – OK, I ran away from The Struggle – as a young, hotshot journalist believing I knew it all. I was one of the first of the adventurous breed who worked on revolutionary *Drum* magazine and created what nostalgia now terms "the golden age of black journalism". I had to know it all to survive in a fast and hard-living society that didn't forgive mistakes but exploited them. I was, in township slang, a klevah: one of the "wake-up" majita on the inside track – a denizen of Jo'burg, Jozi, Gauteng, Egoli.

We took our pick of a favourite name for the city of gold because that choice marked who you were. An insider, outsider or on the fringes of a violent, multiracial society. Some insisted they were European without ever having been there, some of us were classified natives, but warned the land wasn't our own, others were termed coloured as if the rest didn't have any colour. Outsiders fresh out of the bundu were moegoes. "Jim Comes to Jo'burg" types as portrayed in the seminal movie of that title: wide-eyed and marvelling at skyscrapers and the many wonders of a fabled city.

I thought I knew it all until decades later, when it was

Township Life

safe to return home to a land that was about to be our own. Then I realised that this once-upon-a-time klevah was now as ignorant as those Jims. I'd never really known much about the city — nobody ever had, I realised, and that was a reason for the various names for this economic capital of the country.

My knowledge of the city as a wake-up majita of the Kofifi era was really only a blinkered view of one part of society. And I had abandoned that in favour of even greater cities north of the equator. Now I have the freedom to explore and actually live in those enclaves where once the only black people tolerated were domestic servants. In the old days, we could only glimpse the suburbs we called "the avenues" in the light of day. We saw luxurious houses on tree-lined streets on the routes our commuter buses thundered along into the city. And all we knew of that city was what was necessary for us to hustle for tiny bits of the gold that was supposed to pave the streets.

We didn't know "the real" Jo'burg of verdant valleys above the gold reefs that bulged into ridges, hills and rocky koppies. We didn't know the quiet, tree-lined streets that were "white by night" and restful, scenic panoramas at all times. What we knew as officially mere "temporary sojourners" were flat, treeless dustbowls once called "locations" before their upliftment to "townships" by apartheid's spin doctors.

The townships and shack non-cities have mushroomed in my absence. Soweto was my final home but is now at least a dozen times larger than the Orlando I roamed before exile, when squatters lived in Masakeng – shacks made of sacking and much more miserable than us living in matchbox houses. But now I'm a moegoe who gets lost in those exclusive enclaves and the city centre amazed this returnee: it boasts real skyscrapers instead of the thirteen-storey Anstey's Building that was once the pride of Jo'burg. That solitary structure was replaced by the Carlton Centre that claimed to be the tallest in Africa.

All my remembered landmarks have disappeared as completely as the Sophiatown we called Kofifi with rundown shops and slum housing. The new danger is not being arrested or mugged but driving against several lines of fast-moving traffic along streets with familiar names that are now one-way thoroughfares.

On my second return in 1994 the president of a democratic state was Nelson Mandela and a white friend remarked: "It's different now, isn't it? A real African city!"

The city of gold had turned black. There were hardly any white faces on streets which teemed with Africans weaving their tricky way around vendors who clogged the pavements. Eloff Street was no longer the main drag once lined by the smartest stores on the continent. They had fled to the suburban shopping malls where white residents live in voluntary exile, fearing the violent crime waves which drown the old central business area. What had once glittered with apparitions of gold had, as some of these internal exiles would say, gone to the dogs. But crime has followed them to Sandton City and other new centres of choice for the best in life.

But there is hopeful transformation too: black sub-urbanites and children of different colours and races are schoolmates and making friendships that are personal and not simply a result of enforced political correctness. I'm still puzzled by white women leading black toddlers by the hand in shopping malls and carrying babies on their hips. Are these children – "piccaninnies" of my own youth – adopted or the offspring of madam's maid? Such a madam would never have dared be seen doing that in the days before her own liberation.

Vocabulary

1 self-imposed (adj.): a self-imposed rule, condition, responsibility etc is one that you have made yourself accept, and which no one has asked you to accept - **2 hotshot** (adj.): *infml.* s.o. who is very successful and confident - **10 denizen** (n.): *literary* an animal, plant, or person that lives or is found in a particular space - **19 seminal** (adj.): a seminal book, piece of music etc is new and important and influences the way in which literature, music etc develops in the future - **30 blinkered** (adj.): having a limited view of a subject or refusing to accept or consider ideas that are new or different - **41 verdant** (adj.): *literary* verdant land is covered with freshly growing green grass and plants - **48 spin doctor** (n.): *infml.* s.o. whose job it is to give information to the public in a way that gives the best possible advantage to a politician or organization - **52 to roam** (v.): to walk or travel, usually for a long time, with no clear purpose or direction - **73 thoroughfare** (n.): the main road through a place such as a city or village - **79 to teem with s.th.** (phr. v.): to be full of people, animals etc - **81 main drag** (n.): *infml.* the main street in a town or city where big shops and businesses are - **86 apparition** (n.): s.th. that you imagine you can see, esp. the spirit of a dead person

Explanations

(Note: *tsotsitaal:* urban slang, language used by gangsters in the townships) - **9 klevah**: *(tsotsitaal)* young men in the cities who are clever and experienced enough to handle the life on the streets - **9 majita**: *(tsotsitaal)* boys, men, friends - **18 bundu**: *(tsotsitaal)* bush, remote rural area - **18 moegoe**: *(tsotsitaal)* ignoramus, derogatory term - **30 Kofifi**: nickname for Sophiatown, a suburb of Johannesburg that was demolished in the 1950s - **43 koppie**: South African expression for a hill - **49 township, Soweto**: see p. 28 - **52 Orlando**: part of Soweto - **53 Masakeng**: township name, now Orlando West - **75 Nelson Mandela**: see p. 27 - **88 Sandton City**: shopping mall in Sandton. Sandton is a northern suburb of Johannesburg - **96 piccaninny**: derogatory term for a small African or aboriginal child.

Actor Sol Rachido with an edition of Drum

Info

Drum magazine

Drum was established in the 1950s and had its headquarters in Johannesburg. Anthony Sampson, Sylvester Stein and Tom Hopkinson worked as editors for the magazine. It contained a mixture of politicised articles and tabloid news about stars, the music industry and sports and gave a voice to the urbanised black population. In addition, it enabled African writers, such as Lewis Nkosi, Can Themba, Nat Nakasa, Es'kia Mphahlele and Arthur Maimane among others, to publish their fiction. These writers also worked as journalists for *Drum*. Other important names attached to the magazine are Henry Nxumalo, Bloke Modisane, Casey Motsisi and Todd Matshikiza. This creative period in the 1950s is referred to as Sophiatown Renaissance. Three well known photographers also started their careers at *Drum*: Jürgen Schadeberg, Bob Gosani and Peter Magubane. After the destruction of Sophiatown in 1955/6 and most of its writers going into exile, *Drum* lost its significance.

Awareness

1 Describe the area or region in which you live. What special landmarks are there?

Comprehension

2 Find the synonyms for Johannesburg in the text.
3 Why does the writer use so many synonyms for the city?
4 What does the writer mean by "the Struggle"?

Analysis

5 How, according to the writer, was the city perceived in the past?
6 How does it contrast with today's impression?
7 How does the writer characterise himself?
8 Characterise the tone of the writing.

Opinion

9 Why does Maimane use tsotsitaal in the text?

Internet Projects

10 Find out more about Johannesburg (see: http://www.joburg.org.za/). The city is often described as being dangerous. Do you think that this is a fair description of the metropolis?
11 "Kofifi" or Sophiatown was an unusual suburb of Johannesburg in the 1940s and 1950s. Find out more about it. What is Sophiatown's history? Why did it become famous?

21

K. Sello Duiker

The Quiet Violence of Dreams

Cape Town is situated at the tip of the African continent and is a well known and popular tourist destination. The "Mother City" was also one of the oldest towns established by the first European settlers in South Africa. For South Africans and international tourists it is the most European city that you will find in the country. The most visible landmark of the town is Table Mountain towering impressively over the city bowl and the harbour. Cape Town is the setting for K. Sello Duiker's novel *The Quiet Violence of Dreams* (2001). It gives a multi-layered insight into the metropolis and functions as an important background for the development of the protagonist Tshepo. – K. Sello Duiker: *The Quiet Violence of Dreams* (Cape Town: Kwela, 2001), pp. 34f., 420.

A shopping area in Kapstadt

I fantasise about taking a walk in Sea Point and think about what Mmabatho said about the whole colour thing. When you go out in some places in Cape Town no one really cares that you're black and that your mother sent you to a private school so that you could speak well. No one cares that you're white and that your father abuses his colleagues at work and calls them kaffirs at home. On the dance floor it doesn't matter which party you voted for in the last election or whether you know how many provinces make up the country. People only care that you can dance and that you look good. They care that you are wearing Soviet jeans with an expensive Gucci shirt and that you have a cute ass. […] They want to see you wearing Diesel jeans with a retro shirt and Nike tackies. They want to see how creatively you can fuse mall shopping with flea market crawling and still remain stylish. Designer labels are the new Esperanto. […] They want to live out their Trainspotting odyssey of excess in a culture rapidly blurring the borders between the township and the northern suburbs. The people I know never forget that in essence the difference between kwaito and rave is down to a difference in beats per minute and that the margin is becoming narrower. It's not that it's fashionable to be seen going out with a person of a different colour. For Mmabatho it seems to be about exploring another culture. Some people are just sick of the expected. Me Tarzan, you Jane has become monotonous. People want to make their own references about who they are and where they fit in or not. It's not enough to simply offer them certain variables, hoping that they'll fit in there somewhere. And Cape Town is not what it used to be. Foreigners have left their imprint on our culture.

Like every growing metropolis Cape Town aspires to be the next best thing. And why shouldn't it? It has a lot going for it. The burgeoning modelling agencies, the politicians who act like celebrities, the scandals, the crude flaunting of money – they all point to a city that wants to be New York, London or Paris. People want to be seen eating croissants at a chic coffee shop at the Table View, rollerblading in Clifton or going for aromatherapy in bohemian Observatory. People want to see you drinking Valpré while working out at the Health & Racquet, with a personal trainer fashionably at your disposal. You must drive an Audi A4 and watch what you eat if you're going to wear your Speedo. You should rather wear Ray Bans than some cheap flea market knock off so that when people see you they must have something that they can relate to past the obvious. Isn't this the fodder advertisers feed us? […] So that colour becomes secondary to the person you present. They want to say ah you're cool and not ah you're black or white. You must be into drumming, support world debt relief and have your chart done.You must know what heita means, what magents are and how to shake hands the African way. You must know what a barmitzvah is, in which direction Mecca faces and who charras are. And which Thai foods go best with soya sauce. You must know all these things and more in a culture pushing to be hybrid and past gender and racial lines. You must aspire for the universality of Ck One and still you must be willing to absorb more. […] These are things that define the club culture in Cape Town, not racial politics.

When I'm with Mmabatho and we talk about growing up in Jo'burg it seems we can only speak in Sotho. Our memories and experiences are too rooted in the township and its language is black. But when we talk about Cape Town or a new bar to go to we find ourselves talking in

English more than Sotho. Cape Town is very white, the influence of European traditions like coffee shops and bistros is inescapable. In some places in Cape Town you don't feel like you're in Africa. And this is what they call progress, obliterate any traces of the native cultures. Jo'burg is different, the other cultures more aggressive to the domination of white culture. I think that has something to do with a bigger, more established black middle class than in Cape Town. Going out in Jo'burg is more pleasant, it isn't such a process of elimination to find a suitable place to enjoy yourself. In Cape Town there are certain places where you know you are not welcome and the patrons make you feel like an outcast. The culture of having a good time, of jolling is different in Gauteng. In Jo'burg people hang out. In Cape Town people go out. In Jo'burg people are into dancing, clothes and what's fashionable. In Cape Town people are into drumming, doing their charts and doing drugs. Cape Town tries too hard, it looks too much to the West for inspiration when there is enough inspiration in Africa.

[...] Most people look at people who live in Jo'burg with a bit of awe or horror, it is difficult to tell sometimes. But what is clear is that the idea of living in a city plagued by violence, high murder and rape statistics, house break-ins, hi-jackings, where personal safety is an issue that everyone faces, leaves a dark image in the mind.

Vocabulary

13 ass (n.): an impolite word for the part of your body that you sit on - **17 Esperanto** (n.): an artificial language invented in 1871 to help people from different countries in the world speak to each other - **34 to aspire** (v.): to desire and work towards achieving s.th. important - **36 burgeoning** (adj.): increasing or developing very quickly - **38 crude** (adj.): offensive or rude, esp. in a sexual way - **38 to flaunt** (v.): to show your money, success, beauty etc so that other people notice it - **50 fodder** (n.): food for farm animals - **73 obliterate** (v.): to destroy s.th. so completely that no sign of it remains

Explanations

1 Sea Point: popular suburb of Cape Town - **2 Mmabatho**: Tshepo's closest friend - **7 kaffir**: derogatory term for Africans (see p. 5) - **15 tackies**: South African English for trainers - **18 Trainspotting**: the title of a novel by Scottish writer Irvine Welsh. The novel focuses on the lives of a few young protagonists and takes the reader into the underworld of Edinburgh. The novel was turned into a successful film in 1996. - **21 kwaito**: music genre that came from Johannesburg in the 1990s. It is part of the youth culture in South Africa. - **27 Me Tarzan, you Jane**: Tarzan is the protagonist of a series of novels by Edgar Rice Burroughs. These lines were supposedly said by Tarzan, but never in fact uttered by him in the books - **43 Valpré**: South African brand for bottled drinking water. It belongs to the Coca Cola Company. - **44 Health & Racquet**: international Fitness club with branches in South Africa - **46 Speedo**: swimwear brand - **47 Ray Bans**: brand of high quality sunglasses - **48 knock off**: fake products - **54 to have your chart done**: to have an astrological chart made showing the influence of the sun, moon and planets on your life - **54 heita**: an informal greeting in South Africa used for expressing happiness when you meet friends or acquaintances - **55 magents**: a brand name for clothing - **57 charras**: derogatory term for Indians. In India "churras" or "charas" means marijuana. - **61 Ck One**: perfume by designer Calvin Klein; brand name - **65 Sotho**: one of the eleven official languages. Language spoken by the Basotho people - **82 jolling**: (South African slang) the term means to have fun or to play.

K. Sello Duiker was born in Orlando West (Soweto) in 1974. He studied journalism and art history at the Rhodes University in Grahamstown where he obtained a B.A. He worked as a scriptwriter for the South African soap operas *Isidingo* and *Backstage*. He became known in the literary scene with the publication of his debut novel *thirteen cents* (2000) in which he portrays the life of a street child in Cape Town. His second novel *The Quiet Violence of Dreams* (2001) is also set in Cape Town and explores the multicultural society in the metropolis. He committed suicide in January 2005. His last novel *The Hidden Star* was published posthumously in 2006.

Awareness

1 How many of the brands and fashion labels mentioned are you familiar with? What do you think are the reasons for their popularity?
2 Which brands, food, and clothing etc are important among your friends?

Comprehension

3 What is meant by the "colour thing" (l. 2)?
4 Why does Cape Town, according to the text, want to be like other cities (l. 39)?
5 Explain what the writer means when he writes that "designer labels are the new Esperanto" (l. 17).
6 Explain what is meant by "a culture pushing to be hybrid" (ll. 59 f.).

Analysis

7 Why, according to the text, are fashion and brands so important in Cape Town?

8 What is meant by "Trainspotting odyssey of excess" (l. 18)?

9 Analyse the comparison the writer makes between Cape Town and Johannesburg. How does he describe the two cities? What is the function of this comparison? What differences between them are highlighted?

Opinion

10 Why does Tshepo stress that he speaks Sotho with his friend Mmabatho in connection with Johannesburg?

11 Why, according to the text, is Cape Town called a "white" city (see l. 69)?

Project

12 Find out more about Cape Town and write an advertisement for travellers in which you praise the tourist highlights of the city and its surroundings. What highlights for tourists can you find?

22

Christopher Saunders / Nicholas Southey

Sports in South Africa*

As in other countries sports play an important role in the life of South Africans either as a hobby or as entertainment on TV or live in a stadium. Cricket, rugby and soccer (football) are very popular in South Africa. After the establishment of democracy, South Africa was able to re-enter the international sports scene and compete with other national teams. Its national rugby team, the Springboks, was especially successful, winning in the World Cup final against the All Blacks, the team from New Zealand, in 1995 and against England in 2007. – Christopher Saunders / Nicholas Southey: *A Dictionary of South African History* (Claremont: David Philip, 2001), pp.161-164.

Modern sport – with its emphasis on physical prowess, self-discipline, individual and collective effort, as well as team competitions, carrying the various communal identities of local district, province and nation – was brought to South Africa in the 19th century by British immigrants. Sport and British cultural values were closely intertwined, and the development of sport reflected the emerging colonial society and its social structures. Although the first recorded cricket match was played in Cape Town in 1808, cricket clubs were slow to form in the Cape before the 1870s. Port Elizabeth saw the establishment of both the first cricket club for whites in 1843 and that for blacks in 1869. Cricket took root in English-speaking public schools and in mission schools in the Cape; by the 1870s, the game was popular throughout the Cape and Natal, although no official leagues or competitions took place. In 1888, the first tour by an English team saw South Africa join England and Australia as a recognized contestant in international cricket,

The emblem of the international cricket team of South Africa called "Proteas"

South Africa wins the Rugby World Cup for the second time in 2007. The Springboks carry the then president Thabo Mbeki on their shoulders

Zola Budd on the fast track

Nelson Mandela congratulates the captain of the Springbok team, Francois Pienaar, for winning the Rugby World Cup in 1995

and further impetus was given to the game in 1890, when Sir Donald Currie donated a trophy, called the Currie Cup, to promote first-class competitive cricket, between the colonies and the republics.

The first rugby match was played in Cape Town in 1862, after which rugby began to spread in schools. [...] In 1891 the South African Rugby Board was founded to ensure uniformity in rules and to organize tournaments and overseas visits; in that year, the first tour by a British team took place. A trophy donated by Sir Donald Currie, which was first competed for in 1892, became the premier inter-provincial award. In 1892, the South African Football Association (SAFA) was formed to control the sport. At the same time, black sportsmen also began to initiate moves to co-ordinate competition on a national level: the South African Coloured Rugby Board was formed in 1896, and the South African Coloured Cricket Board in 1902; black rugby players competed for the Rhodes Cup from 1897 and cricket players for the Barnato trophy from 1898 [...]. At the beginning of the 20th century, cricket was the most popular sport among the small black middle class, and competition between black and white cricket (as well as rugby) teams occurred regularly, particularly in the Cape.

After 1910, however, with the intensification of racism and segregation that occurred as the century progressed, contests between black and white teams declined, along with the assimilationist ideals of the black middle class. The powerful mining industry began to control the development of black sport, and cricket went into decline in favour of working-class mass sports, in particular soccer, boxing and athletics. Cricket tended to be associated in popular discourse as the sport of English-speaking whites, while rugby came to be dominated by Afrikaners. After 1948, the apartheid policies of the National Party stretched, not surprisingly, to the sporting arena. In 1955, the government published its official sports policy based on racial differentiation: each race was to have its own sports amenities, controlling bodies, emblems, and local and international competitions. By the end of the 1950s, this official policy of sport apartheid was making its influence felt in almost every sporting code. Between 1959 and 1962, several black federations, in cricket, football, tennis and athletics, made a transition towards non-racialism; in 1962, the most influential of these, the South African Non-Racial Olympic Committee (SANROC), was formed. Under the leadership of Sam Ramsamy it established itself in exile in London in 1966, and led campaigns to isolate South Africa on the sportsfield.

The international boycott of South African sport, although unevenly applied, increasingly made an impact on the white establishment. South Africa was expelled from international football in 1964, from the Olympic Games in 1966 and the Olympic movement in 1969, and from international cricket in 1970 [...]. The unyielding attitude of the government was symbolized most clearly in its refusal to grant permission to Basil D'Oliveira, a Coloured cricketer of South African birth, to participate in a cricket test series between England and South Africa in 1966. This was the same year in which a Department of Sport and Recreation was established to influence the practice of sport in the country.

In 1973, the South African Council of Sport (SAGOS) was formed within the country, and, together with SANROC, campaigned for the complete isolation of South African sport, using the Slogan "no normal sport in an abnormal society". [...] During the 1980s, the sports boycott was applied with considerable effectiveness, with only rugby and some individual sportspeople succeeding in evading isolation to any significant degree. Opponents of international tours argued that sport should rather be developed in disadvantaged communities. [...]

Campaigners had long argued that the use of sport in isolating white South Africa was an extremely effective psychological weapon in the broader antiapartheid struggle, and the termination of the rebel cricket tour was a significant landmark in popular domestic opposition to apartheid. In November 1990, a broad coalition of opposition sporting organizations decided in Harare that the sports boycott should remain in place until the scrapping of apartheid. [...] The isolation of cricket ended in October 1991, with a short tour of the national team to India, and an invitation to the World Cup in Australia in March 1992. South African sportspeople then performed with credit in international competition: the country reached the semifinals of the cricket World Cup in 1992, was victorious in the rugby World Cup in 1995, and in the soccer Africa Cup of Nation in 1996; at the 1996 Olympics, Josiah Thugwane won the gold medal in the men's marathon.

These successes have not disguised considerable challenges facing many sports in the post-apartheid era: the allocation of resources, vastly diverse facilities, and the virtual absence of Africans in many national teams are among the major issues which confront sporting bodies.

Vocabulary

1 prowess (n.): *fml.* great skill at doing s.th. - **79 amenity** (n.): s.th. such as a piece of equipment, shop, or park that makes it easier to live somewhere - **129 landmark** (n.): an event, idea or discovery that marks an important part of s.o.'s life, of the development of knowledge etc

Explanations

Introduction: **Soccer**: note that the South Africans use the US-American term for football (BrE) - **33 Sir Donald Currie** (1825-1909): British shipowner. He decided to run a steamer service between Great Britain and the Cape Colony which later became known as the Union-Castle lines. - **56 Rhodes Cup**: Cup donated by Sir Cecil Rhodes (1853-1902). Rhodes was a British imperialist, mining magnate and politician. - **57 Barnato trophy**: trophy donated by Barney Barnato (1852-1897). He was a diamond magnate. - **76 National Party**: see p. 35 - **87 Sam Ramsamy** (*1938): South African activist and sports administrator - **141 Josiah Thugwane**: marathon athlete who won a gold medal at the Olympic Games in Atlanta in 1996.

Awareness

1 What is the most popular sport in your country? Is it also your favourite sport, or do you prefer other sports? Explain why you like or dislike certain sports.

Comprehension

2 When were rugby and cricket clubs established in South Africa?
3 Which racial group preferred which sports at the beginning of the 20th century?

Analysis

4 How did cricket develop in South Africa?
5 How were sports affected by apartheid?

Opinion

6 Should sports be used as a political weapon? If so, how should they be used and if not, why not?

Project

7 Zola Budd (see p. 61) was a South African athlete in the 1980s. Her special case was well-known around the world. Find out more about Zola Budd. In which sport and for which country did she compete?

23

Phaswane Mpe

"An Ode to Bafana Bafana"

Soccer (football) is among the most popular sports in South Africa. It is a sport of the people that is mainly played in the streets and stadiums of the townships. South Africa's national team is called "Bafana Bafana". Though it did not qualify for the last World Cup in Germany in 2006, South Africa hosts the next one in 2010. Stadiums have been rebuilt or newly built in every major town or city all over the country. Phaswane Mpe (see p. 49) wrote a poem about the international team of South Africa in 1998 called "An Ode to Bafana Bafana". – Phaswane Mpe: *Brooding Clouds*, Scottsville/RSA: University of KwaZulu-Natal Press, 2008, pp. 168, 70.

ai

we sang...
we sang shosholoza
sent you off with rhymes
of joy & hope stifled
by our knowledge of your youth
in matters of world cups
we brooded over the deprivations
& depravities of apartheid
of amabokoboko
beating ireland with scores
of fists that frightened the irish
made them fearful
of scoring their own goals
to fill oceans of nationhood
flowing within their literature
james joyce forgot about the artist
as a young man
& focused his sharp gaze
on you bafana bafana
playing your first round like boys
stranded in a zoo
of noisy spectators screaming au revoir
benny mccarthy magic
& no wonder boys
there was no madiba magic
spurring you on from the maddening crowds
of noises of shosholoza
uprooted from its south african soil
& stranded in the green lands [...]
you lost bafana bafana
but we knew you were stimela's franky
wanting to go to the city
it is enticing & menacing that hillbrow
that you would go to
softly now boys...
tread softly as you wade your way
towards 2002
a big leap towards 2006 and beyond
when we might watch from heavens
as you soar like eagles [...]

Pure joy of life: Bafana fans at the first game of the Confederations Cup, 14 June 2009

Vocabulary

8 deprivation (n.): s.th. you need or usually have that you are prevented from having - **9 to deprave** (v.): *fml.* to be an evil influence on s.o., esp. s.o. who is young or not very experienced - **34 enticing** (adj.): very pleasant or interesting so that you feel strongly attracted - **34 menacing** (adj.): making you expect s.th. unpleasant - **37 wade** (v.): to walk through water that is not deep

Explanations

Introduction: **bafana**: means "boys", the name of the national soccer team - **1 ai**: exclamation of surprise, pain or dismay - **3 shosholoza**: popular South African "working song" sung at rugby matches by Springbok supporters - **10 amabokoboko**: African name for the international rugby team - **11 beating Ireland**: South Africa beat Ireland in two Rugby test matches in 1998. The results were 37-13 and 33-0. These were devastating defeats for the Irish. - **17 James Joyce** (1882-1941): Irish writer. He wrote the novels *Ulysses* (1922) and *A Portrait of the Artist as a Young Man* (1916), among other important works. - **24 Benny McCarthy**: popular South African soccer player - **26 Madiba**: affectionate nickname for Nelson Mandela (see p. 27) - **32 stimela**: popular South African jazz group headed by Ray Phiri - **32 Franky**: an allusion to US-American singer and actor Frank Sinatra (1915-1998) - **34 Hillbrow**: see p. 47

Awareness

1 Do you know any players in the South African football team? Do you know any South African players in Germany? Who are they, and which teams do they play for?

Comprehension

2 What is the name of the national rugby team given in the poem?

Analysis

3 What is an ode? Why does Mpe use the form of an ode?
4 What literary devices can you find in the poem? What is their function in the poem?
5 Why does the poet mention a) James Joyce (l. 17) b) Franky (l. 32)?
6 What is meant by "madiba magic" (l. 26)?

Opinion

7 How important is football (soccer) in your country? Do you think it is overrated? Give reasons for your opinion.

Projects

8 Imagine the final of the World Cup (2010 or later) is your national team against Bafana Bafana. Write a newspaper article or radio report about the game.
9 Find out about the two most famous South African soccer teams: Orlando Pirates and Kaizer Chiefs (http://www.orlandopiratesfc.com/ and http://www.kaizerchiefs.com/).
a) What do they have in common? b) Which other nicknames do they have and what do they mean? c) How are they seen by their supporters? Explain why their supporters view the teams as they do.